Thomas Welbank Fowle

The Poor Law

Thomas Welbank Fowle

The Poor Law

ISBN/EAN: 9783744791557

Printed in Europe, USA, Canada, Australia, Japan

Cover: Foto ©Suzi / pixelio.de

More available books at **www.hansebooks.com**

BY

T. W. FOWLE, M.A.

RECTOR OF ISLIP

𝔏𝔬𝔫𝔡𝔬𝔫

MACMILLAN AND CO., Limited

NEW YORK: THE MACMILLAN COMPANY

1898

First Edition 1881
Second Edition 1890.   *Reprinted* 1893, 1898

PREFACE TO THE SECOND EDITION.

IN a series of books such as the *English Citizen* it is, I think, best to suppress the individuality of the author as much as possible; and beyond saying that this edition of this book is the same as the former, with some verbal alterations, and an appendix bringing down the subject to the present date, I should not have thought it worth while to write a formal preface. But I cannot lose the opportunity of acknowledging, with due thanks, the even more than usual German thoroughness with which Dr. Aschrott, in his late German book on the Poor Law, has appropriated this book of mine—treating it, in short, as a kind of German Hinterland; and of assuring him in all seriousness that so far as I have helped him to expound the mysteries of English Poor Law to his countrymen I am quite content. Perhaps, however, the case is a little altered when his book is translated back into English with a preface by no less a person than Professor Henry Sidgwick, containing the stereotyped intimation .that an urgent (English) need has been supplied in a remarkably thorough piece of (German) work. However, I shall not retaliate further than by a delicious illustration of the dangers that await—let us call it—unlicensed appropriation. On p. 77 I quote from Sir F. Head the story of the parish clerk who threatened to fight the overseer if he did not pay him for ringing the bell at paupers' funerals; and on p. 114 I point out that the clerk, *i.e.* of the Guardians, has a "supremacy much greater than is usually held by similar officers." Dr. Aschrott "combines his information" with the following disastrous result (p. 33): "In many instances the clerk was the chief or even the sole actor. In answer to a question why certain improper expenditure had been incurred, an overseer stated, 'Why, sir, the clerk is a dreadful man, and always threatens to fight me whenever I want to stop such a charge.' And if the clerk's physical powers were not usually exercised in this fashion, knowledge and education often made him master of the situation." To the British mind the idea of a respectable country solicitor fighting an overseer is good; better far is the idea of our familiar old friend, the parish clerk, being, by virtue of superior knowledge, master of the situation. Well, after all, I am but a country clergyman, and—perhaps he is.

CONTENTS.

" To provide for us in our necessities is not in the power of Government. It would be a vain presumption in statesmen to think they can do it. The people maintain them, and not they the people. It is in the power of Government to prevent much evil it can do very little positive good in this, or perhaps in anything else. It is not only so of the State and statesman, but of all the classes and descriptions of the rich ; they are the pensioners of the poor, and are maintained by their superfluity. They are under an absolute, hereditary, and indefeasible dependence on those who labour, and are miscalled the poor."—EDMUND BURKE.

THE POOR LAW.

CHAPTER I.

POOR LAW PRINCIPLES.

LEGAL provision for the relief of the destitute is not, like other national institutions, — for instance, Parliament, courts of justice, or a standing army, — a plain and necessary part of civilised social organisation, requiring no explanation and needing no defence. On the contrary, such provision would seem at first sight artificial and even unnatural, for it establishes a state of things in which persons are not obliged, unless they choose, to provide themselves with the means of subsistence; while those who work for their own living are compelled, whether they like it or not, to maintain those who will not or cannot support themselves. Hence it is always found necessary, in treating of this subject, to begin by showing why there ought to be and in point of fact *must* be a Poor Law before we can discuss profitably what Poor Laws ought to be, or describe what they have been. We have, therefore, no choice but to ask the reader's attention to the reasons that have impelled civilized societies to provide for the relief of

destitution at the public cost, in order that he may the
better understand the past history and present arrangements of the Poor Law in his own country.

Even the word "poor" requires explanation. It is
used to describe two different, though allied, classes of
persons,—first, those who are actually destitute ; second,
those who would be destitute but for that manual labour
which constitutes their "property," and is the chief source
of the wealth of mankind. This is what Burke alludes
to in the motto prefixed to this book, when he speaks
of the labouring class as being "miscalled the poor."
Elsewhere the same writer, who never touched upon any
subject that he did not adorn with wise thought and
noble feeling, and who has done far more than any other
man to define and fix the principles of the English Constitution, exclaims, "We have heard many plans for the
relief of the labouring poor. This puling jargon is not
as innocent as it is foolish. Hitherto the name of poor
(in the sense in which it is used to excite compassion)
has not been used for those who can but for those who
cannot labour—for the sick and infirm, for orphan infancy,
for languishing and decrepit age ; but when we affect to
pity, as poor, those who must labour or the world cannot
exist, we are trifling with the condition of mankind. . . .
I do not call a healthy young man, cheerful in his mind
and vigorous in his arms,—I cannot call such a man
poor ; I cannot pity my kind as a kind, merely because
they are men. . . ."—(*Third Letter on a Regicide Peace*).

The same distinction is drawn in the Report of the
Commissioners in 1834 (page 227); but, rather unfortun-
ately, the word "poor" is there used in the sense which
Burke deprecated. Thus "the state of a person unable

to labour, or unable to obtain in return for his labour the means of subsistence" is called "Indigence," and "Poverty" is used to describe "the state of one who, in order to obtain a mere subsistence, is forced to have recourse to labour." In the *Edinburgh Review* for July 1836, the practical evils that resulted from this ambiguity in the use of the word "poor" are very forcibly pointed out, and the practical conclusion thus summed up:—"Indigence may be provided for, mendicity may be extirpated, but all attempts to extirpate poverty can have no effects but bad ones." In the present treatise, therefore, the word will not be used; but words such as indigence, destitution, and the like, will be applied to one class, and the other will be described by the more fitting title of labouring or working people.

There is another popular misapprehension, which, though exposed nearly fifty years ago, still does something more than linger on, even in quarters where more accurate information might be looked for. Noticing the results of the investigation into foreign systems of Poor Law made in 1834, the *Quarterly Review* writes, "We believe that the general impression, till very lately, has been that England stands alone among nations in the provision which her laws have made against destitution. Certainly those who questioned the policy of this institution have continually inveighed against it as one of an extraordinary and unexampled nature; while its advocates have appeared to shrink from supporting their views, as they might have done, by a reference to the fact that *its principle has long since been adopted by all really civilized communities.*" Although this investigation was repeated upon a most extensive scale in 1874, and its

results embodied in a volume which is the authority for
all statements concerning foreign Poor Laws contained in
this treatise, it is very doubtful whether the public mind
is at all disabused of the mistake. The existence of
pauperism in England is still very frequently set down
to some national peculiarity, whether for evil or good,
according to the taste of the writer, such as our system
of land laws, or our superiority in the virtue of social
benevolence. No doubt, in the English Poor Law, as in
other national institutions, there are some very strongly
defined characteristics, most of which, it may be here
said, redound to our credit as compared with other countries rather than the reverse. But the fact is that in all
civilized countries the same kind of difficulties concerning
the support of the indigent have been encountered, the
same sort of remedies been tried, and the same experi-
ences, mostly of a painful and disappointing character,
been gone through. Two or three facts in proof of this
may be adduced. Belgium has been called upon good
authority the "classic land of Pauperism." In France
the immediate result of the Revolution of 1789 was
to substitute for the system of public benevolence then
existing a system of support founded upon legal rights,
which, however, only lasted four or five years. Holland
has tried the latest and perhaps the most advanced experiment in Poor Law legislation no longer ago than 1870.
Finally, there are elaborate systems of poor relief in the
United States, with the result that in the typical State of
Massachusetts the amount of pauperism in proportion
to population was recently calculated at considerably
more than one half of that existing in England.[1]

[1] See reports communicated to the Local Government Board in

What, then, is the "principle" that makes the institution of Poor Laws a necessary part of social organisation? Out of many answers that have been given to this question there are two which, though inadequate, have played so important a part in the history of Poor Law, and have given rise to so much interesting discussion, that they cannot be passed over in silence. They may be called the "sentimental" and "utilitarian" reasons respectively: the first, that all men have a natural right to the means of existence; the second, that society is compelled, in the interests of its own self-preservation, to take some care of destitute persons. Both these propositions are, in a certain sense, true, though not so as to answer the question before us.

The first or sentimental reason is expressed in such phrases as the following:—"The right of every peaceful and obedient member of society to the means of subsistence;" or, "It is an admitted maxim of social polity that the first charge on land must always be the maintenance of the people reared upon it. This is the principle of the English Poor Law" (Nicholls's *History of the Poor Law*, vol. i. p. 2). This last opinion is very commonly held and positively affirmed, but to estimate its true value we have but to remember that no man from the moment of his birth can enforce any claim to any "rights" except what some one or other, or society itself, chooses to allow him; and, again, that if we start from the rights of individuals, it is impossible to draw a line between things which are and things which are not "natural" rights. But it is more to the purpose to

1875, with preface by Mr. Doyle, and special reports as to Holland and the United States by Mr Sendall and Mr. Henley respectively.

point out that this so-called right has been peremptorily
denied, and the denial even erected into a maxim of
State policy.   Thus it has been said, "There is no
danger of which foreign legislation" (the allusion is more
especially to France) "appears to be more apprehensive
than the recognition of any right of working men to be
relieved, or even to have work found for them when
destitute.   They are relieved, but always with the reser-
vation that such aid is given not of right but of charity"
(Doyle, p. 6).   And M. Thiers has further laid down the
principle "that when the virtue of charity ceases to be
private, and becomes collective, it is essential that it
should preserve its character of a virtue,—that is to say,
that it should remain voluntary and spontaneous; for
otherwise it would cease to be a virtue, and would
become a dangerous compulsion."   On the other hand,
the necessity of some provision for relief of indigence is
so manifest that one French minister enunciated the
proposition "that no one has a right to public relief, but
that the bestowal of such relief is a duty incumbent on
the State."   This, which the author of the report calls a
somewhat "illogical statement of the case," nevertheless
approximates, as we shall see, closely to the true principle of Poor Laws.—(*Report of the Relief of the Poor in
France*, by E. Lee Hamilton, p. 136.)

It may be interesting to note the different positions
which various nations have taken up in respect of the
"right" to maintenance.   Sweden in 1870, Denmark in
1866, re-enacting a law of 1683, and Prussia in 1871,
have expressly conferred upon all destitute persons the
right to such relief as is necessary.   Holland in 1870
framed a new Poor Law, in which it was expressly laid

down that "no person has a right to relief, and that the care of the poor is a moral not a civil duty; that the exercise of charity should be relegated to the Church or to private charity; but that where these agencies do not exist it may become necessary for the State to intervene in the interests of public decency and order," which is only arriving at the same point by a different way. France in 1793 formally declared that the relief of the destitute was a national debt, but retraced her steps five years later from experience of the evils entailed, — a measure which included Belgium also. England, followed in this by the United States, occupies an intermediate and, it would seem, more intelligible position. Nothing is said about the rights of persons to receive relief, but the duty is cast upon localities to see that no person perishes for want of the means of existence. There is, therefore, no right that can be enforced by legal process; but Lord Chief-Justice Cockburn laid it down that there ought to be some remedy if a destitute person is refused relief, either by indictment, or, preferably, by mandamus (Glen, *Poor Law Orders*, p. 62). The same rule appears to obtain in Austria and some German States, an appeal being allowed to a higher authority than the parish in at least one State (Baden). It may be adduced as a curious proof how practically the most extreme theories end in the same results, that in Holland, until the year 1854, liability to repayment of relief might be enforced against charitable institutions, the point having been decided against them in several instances.—(Sendall, p. 20.)

The plain truth is, that theories which start from the rights or status of individuals lead us at last nowhere in determining the principles upon which societies must and ought to act. We have only to push the theory to its extreme limits and see what we should come to. Thus an Englishman might very fairly urge that the want of any recognised title to relief would, under certain circumstances, produce a Revolution, and that, as a matter of fact, the French Revolution was largely caused by the existence of indigence driven to despair by the hopelessness of relief. And a Frenchman might, with equal justice, retort that the bestowal of a legal right to relief would, under certain circumstances, lead to practical Communism, as it had done in England at the time of the Poor Law Reform of 1834.

The second or utilitarian principle has been stated in its naked and somewhat revolting common sense as follows :—" Whenever, for the purposes of Government, we arrive in any state of society at a class so miserable as to be in want of the common necessaries of life, a new principle comes into action. The usual restraints, which are sufficient for the well-fed, are often useless in checking the demands of hungry stomachs. Hence . . . it may be expedient, in a merely economical point of view, to supply gratuitously the wants of even able-bodied persons, if it can be done without creating crowds of additional applicants."—(Babbage, *Principles of Taxation*, quoted by Nicholls.)

Now this statement contains two undeniable and important truths. It declares that the good of the community, and not the rights of individuals, is the legitimate cause of legal provision for destitution, and it pays regard to the fact that in all countries Poor Law legislation has been devised to meet certain plain and growing evils that were endangering the social fabric. Its error is that it overlooks these moral or humanitarian considerations which are just as necessary to the well-being of society as material or economical conditions, and which would compel the establishment of a system of State relief even could it be shown that as a matter of policy or of economy no such relief was needed. And by separating off the indigent class from the rest of society, it lays itself open to the retort that Poor Laws, so far from being capable of being defended on grounds of general expediency, have always been instituted in the selfish interests of privileged classes. The opinion is attributed to Mr. Nassau Senior that they "originated in ignorance, selfishness, and pride, and in an attempt substantially to restore the expiring system of slavery." Others have expressed the same idea by ascribing Poor Laws to the survival of Feudalism—that is, to the policy which separates the labouring classes from ownership of the land. And finally, the expediency of State relief in the interests of the working people themselves is thus seriously challenged by so eminent an authority as Mr. Malthus :—"I feel persuaded that if Poor Laws had never existed in this country, though there might have been a few more instances of very severe distress, the aggregate mass of happiness among the common people would have been much greater than at present." He ascribes their "tendency to depress the condition of the 'poor'" to four causes,—"the impulse they give to the increase of population without increasing the supply of food," the consumption of food in workhouses by non-workers, the artificial rise in the price of provisions, together with the lowering of the price of labour, so that

"they impoverish the class of people whose only possession is their labour," and "may be said to create the
poor whom they maintain."

This brief survey of the curiously different points of
view from which the provision of State relief has been
regarded by leading authorities will enable the reader to
compare the various opinions that have been held respecting it, and also to apprehend the general principle which,
as being common to all theories concerning it, may be assigned as the actual cause of Poor Law legislation. For all
are agreed, whatever may be the reason they give for their
conclusion, that indigence must be relieved by some one
or other, and at the cost of the community, by whatever
name we choose to call the process by which the relief
is conveyed. This law or fact we may express in the
following terms :—*That every society upon arriving at a
certain stage of civilization finds it positively necessary for its
own sake,—that is to say, for the satisfaction of its own humanity, and for the due performance of the purposes for which
societies exist,—to provide that no person, no matter what has
been his life, or what may be the consequences, shall perish for
want of the bare necessaries of existence.* Even if history
did not make it plain to us, as we shall see when we
come to treat of the origin of Poor Law in England, that
this was the simple matter of fact principle which gave
rise to the institution of State relief, a very slight consideration of what is involved in the idea of a society
would teach us that, in the higher and more delicate types
of social organization, what we might call the moral life
of the community is incompatible with the spectacle of
unrelieved indigence connived at by the comfortable and
prosperous classes. It is precisely the "few more cases

of very severe distress," the possibility of which Mr. Malthus admits, that people feel must be dealt with some- how, and that so as to give a reasonable certainty that there will be nothing to shock our natural feelings of humanity and kindness.   How can men enjoy life with the knowledge that their neighbours are starving?   Or how can a State call upon its citizens to fight for their country, or to tax themselves for such objects as govern- ment, justice, religion, if all these, which are the moral glory of mankind, do not avail to prevent other citizens from dying in the agonies of cold and hunger?   Of nations, as of men, it may be truly said, that if they have not charity they are nothing.

The actual condition of things out of which this feeling of humanity struggled into existence was the embarrassment men felt in punishing (with frightful penalties) vagrancy and mendicancy, or even crime itself, without affording some assurance that the bodily wants which drive persons to these courses were not altogether unprovided for at the public cost.   Moreover, as the social conscience became more mature, there arose a dim and indistinct feeling that pauperism and crime were due to inherited conditions of moral and physical evil, for which paupers and criminals were in no sense responsible, but which had to a large extent grown out of the selfish neglect or mischievous ignorance of the nation itself in previous ages.   Who, for instance, that has ever realised the injuries which the labouring classes have endured from State interference with their work and wages, or from State non-interference with their dwellings and surroundings, could, with any peace of conscience, leave those unhappy persons upon whom the curse has fallen to perish in want, disease, or ignorance? The thing is impossible, and because it was found to be impossible, therefore,—apart from all theories and independently of all results,—the public relief of destitution, together with laws for its administration, became a recognised part of the duties undertaken by civilized States.

This reference to the natural operation of humanity, *as a thing due from society to its own self-respect*, is to be found virtually in all the reasons which legislators or writers have assigned as being the principle of Poor Law administration in their respective countries.[1] We shall, however, content ourselves with adducing the authority of Mr. J. S. Mill, whose account of the matter is in agreement with what has been stated above, and will probably, from its directness and simplicity, commend itself to the reader as a satisfactory statement of the facts of the case :—"Apart from any metaphysical considerations respecting the foundation of morals, or of the social union, it will be admitted to be right that human beings should help one another, and the more so in proportion to the urgency of the need ; and none needs help so urgently as one who is starving. The claim to help, therefore, created by destitution is one of the strongest which can exist, and there is *primâ facie* the amplest reason for making the relief of so extreme an exigency as certain to those who require it as by any arrangements of society it can be made."—(*Polit. Economy*, v. xi. 13).

It is worth while to observe how the various theories mentioned above fall into their proper place when once we have a plain matter of fact principle to go upon.

---

[1] It is very clearly stated as the "principle" of poor relief in the report from Massachusetts.—Mr. Henley's Report, p. 78.

Take, for instance, the question of "rights." Every destitute person has a right to relief, not because his "status," *i.e.* his miserable condition, gives him a title to it (which is an obsolete idea suitable only to primitive stages of social growth), but because the State has made for its own purposes a contract to stand between its citizens and death by starvation; for, as it has been well said, every Government enactment securing relief to the indigent is of the nature of a compact between the State and each of its members. And for practical purposes, either by legal relief or organised charity, this right is conferred by every civilized society.

Once more, this principle enables us to draw a clear line between State relief and private charity. The motive of the former is primarily and chiefly the welfare, or, at any rate, the resolution of the giver; whereas charity ceases to be charity if the giver puts his own comfort or interests before the needs of the recipient. Hence there can be no such thing as legal charity, and, melancholy as the assertion may sound, it nevertheless follows that although, of course, all human beings ought to act humanely towards each other, yet we are not to look, in a system of State relief, for moral graces such as gratitude from the recipient, or liberality from the official giver who dispenses other people's money. "Free charity indeed," exclaimed a blunt Dutchman, in a parliamentary debate, "with my neighbour's hand in my pocket!" This distinction may turn out in the future to be of much importance in mapping out the two provinces of legal relief and voluntary charity.

We shall see, when we come to deal with it, how far the history of Poor Laws in England bears out the opinion already alluded to, that they were due neither to humanity nor genuine utilitarianism, but to the interests of mere class selfishness. At present it may be sufficient to observe that the true statement of the case would seem to be that the selfishness of the upper classes took advantage of the growing spirit of humanity, and made a kind of tacit bargain with it, whereby, upon condition that localities provided for the relief of the "impotent," they were authorized to reduce the able-bodied labourer to a state of practical slavery, under the plea of setting him to work. But we have little doubt that the Report of the Committee of the House of Commons in 1817,— viz. "the principle of a compulsory provision for the impotent, and for setting to work the able-bodied, originated in motives of the *purest* humanity,"—contains, with the omission of the word "purest," a true description of the origin of Poor Laws in England. At any rate the motive of humanity, let it have been ever so small, has long survived the interests of selfishness, and may be assigned as the decisive reason why Poor Laws have continued to exist long after they could, with any plausibility, be described as instruments designed to oppress or enslave the labouring classes.

Seeing, then, that societies cannot allow any of their members to perish from preventible causes, the first and main object of Poor Law legislation is plainly to provide a certain maintenance for all indigent persons,—that is, those who, from any cause whatever, have come to such a condition as that, without help, they would die of want. But then, as Mr. Mill goes on to point out, in all cases of helping there are two sets of consequences to be considered,—the consequences of the assistance itself, and the consequences of relying on it. "'The former are generally beneficial, but the latter for the most part injurious." This, indeed, is a very mild statement of the evils which, as a matter of history, have arisen from relying upon the certainty of relief, whether by public law or private charity. We shall endeavour to give some faint idea of them when we come to deal with the old English Poor Law, under which they rose to a height unprecedented, perhaps, except in Belgium. At present we merely indicate the chief sources from which they flow, although in truth they are so subtle, so intricate, and so mixed, that it is difficult to describe them generally, much more to arrange them under heads.

(1.) The knowledge that the necessaries of life can be had for the asking naturally induces men who are not really destitute to throw themselves upon the State for aid. Hence State relief inevitably promotes idleness, with its kindred vices.

(2.) The same knowledge induces men to look forward to being supported by State relief whenever the time shall come that they are really destitute; whence comes dependence, with all the faults that follow in its train.

(3.) The same knowledge quenches the natural sentiment of the human heart towards relatives or friends, the care of whom is thrown off upon the law in place of those to whom it properly belongs. Hence inhumanity and selfishness.

(4.) The provision of State relief, especially if the true principles of social or political economy are not understood, leads to interference with the natural course of trade and employment, besides benefiting particular

interests or localities (generally those who least need it)
at the expense of poorer or weaker neighbours.

If, then, the first great object of Poor Law legislation
be the provision of relief for the destitute, we may properly describe the second object as the prevention of the
evils and abuses that flow from the first. And in point
of fact the history of Poor Laws, down to recent times,
is one long melancholy record of admitted and repeated
failures to deal with evils that recur with monotonous
persistency, or break out in new forms, or evade the
best meant schemes for putting them down. Naturally
enough a mere policy of repression was first attempted,
and by degrees a second principle, which may be almost
called the charter of Poor Law reform, was arrived at,
and is now in theory everywhere admitted, though still
in practice too often sinned against. We take the
description of it from the singularly able report on the
further amendment of the Poor Law in 1839 by Mr.
Lefevre, Sir George Nicholls, and Sir George Cornewall
Lewis, to which we would gladly refer the reader for
full information on the theory and practice of poor
relief, but that it is unfortunately out of print. They
say (p. 45):—

"The fundamental principle with respect to the legal
relief of the poor is, that the condition of the pauper
ought to be, on the whole, less eligible than that of the
independent labourer. The equity and expediency of
this principle are equally obvious. Unless the condition
of the pauper is, on the whole, less eligible than that of
the independent labourer, the law destroys the strongest
motives to good conduct, steady industry, providence,
and frugality among the labouring classes, and induces

persons, by idleness or imposture, to throw themselves upon the poor rates for support. But if the independent labourer sees that a recurrence to the poor rates will, while it protects him against destitution, place him in a less eligible position than that which he can attain to by his own industry, he is left to the undisturbed influence of all those motives which prompt mankind to exertion, forethought, and self-denial. On the other hand, the pauper has no just ground for complaint if at the same time that his physical wants are amply provided for, his condition should be less eligible than that of the poorest class of those who contribute to his support."

In the last clause the two fundamental principles of Poor Laws are brought together, i.e. relief for the destitute, but so as that their condition shall be worse than if they had taken pains to support themselves. There is, however, a third, and, though subsidiary, hardly less important object at which legislation has aimed with but scanty results in different countries. Partly because there are deteriorating effects upon the class which cannot be altogether met by measures directed against abuses by individuals, partly because when once the State has interfered between men and the natural consequences of their own behaviour, it cannot help being drawn into further measures on their behalf, there emerges another object, which may be described as the prevention of the pauperising effects of State relief by measures calculated to raise the condition of the working classes. Thus the description of the objects of legal provision for the support of the poor in Massachusetts is as follows :—" This intervention is generally limited to the relief of absolute necessity to save life or pre-

C

vent disease and suffering. But *incidentally* it aims at
improving the condition of the poor, by teaching and
training the young for work and self-dependence, by
inculcating morality and promoting industry, cleanliness,
and temperance."—(Mr. Henley's Report, p. 78.)

We have thus, then, arrived at the three main objects
which Poor Laws are framed to carry out, and round
which all their various institutions and provisions can be
arranged. These are—

(1.) Relief measures to support the indigent.

(2.) Repressive measures to put down, and

(3.) Remedial measures to prevent, the abuses and
evils which are sure to be engendered by a system of
State relief. By what means men have attempted to
attain each of these three objects will be detailed in the
next chapter.

CHAPTER II.

WE propose in this chapter to enumerate, with such brief description and comparison as is possible, the various institutions, enactments, and arrangements which Poor Laws have called into existence. By way of giving as clear and comprehensive a view as the nature of the subject allows, we shall classify them under the following six heads :—

   I. The Authorities by whom ⎫
  II. The Funds from which   ⎬ relief is administered.
 III. The Persons to whom   ⎪
 IV. The Methods by which   ⎭
   V. Repressive Measures.
 VI. Remedial Measures.

The above classification does not pretend to any scientific accuracy, which, to say truth, would be an almost impossible undertaking : thus the " House " is at once a method of relief and a repressive measure. But the reader will, we trust, be enabled to compare the various forms which poor relief has assumed in different countries, and to discern from what states of society or modes of thinking they have grown up.

Attempts have been made to classify Poor Laws according to the systems that obtain in various nations, but with a success so doubtful that it does not seem worth while to fatigue the memory of the reader by adding another to the list. It must be, however, understood, that there will meet us at every turn a plain, broad distinction between the Teutonic or Scandinavian and Protestant nations of the north, and the Latin and Catholic nations of the south. This makes it all the more to be regretted that there is no available information about the present state of things in Switzerland, except a brief account, as far back as 1834, of the Canton of Berne, where things appear to have been as bad as they were in England at that time, and from much the same causes.—(Mr. Morier's Report. See *Quarterly Review* for December 1835, which contains a brief summary of the Reports from foreign countries.)

As our object is to gain a general idea of what Poor Law has been and has done, before entering into the details of English legislation, we shall allude to the latter as little as possible in this chapter, reserving it for fuller treatment hereafter.

I. *The Authorities by whom poor relief is administered.*—As the way in which the various authorities— local (*i.e.* parochial, or communal), municipal, provincial, and central—came to be concerned in the administration of Poor Law, is a matter of historical growth, we may divide the history roughly into three periods : that before the Reformation, that between the Reformation and the French Revolution, and lastly, the ninety years that have elapsed since that event. In the first period there was virtually no Poor Law at all, only a series of enactments, horrible in their revolting severity against pauperism, especially in the form of vagrancy ; and another series, if possible, more detestable, against the rights of free labour. But the indigent and miserable were left to the care of the Church, which, it must be confessed, was rich enough and powerful enough to make it certain that relief in some shape would be forthcoming to those who needed it. The monasteries afforded food and shelter to the mendicant, and something like out-relief to the destitute inhabitants of the districts in which they were placed. There was also a claim upon lords of the manor for the maintenance of their dependants, a state of things which survived in Russia until the year 1864. Something, too, was done by trade guilds towards the support of their own members, traces of which,—as for instance in the case of the London companies,—still remain. But for a genuine survival of mediæval arrangements we must look to the Turkish empire, in which (Mahomet having exhorted his people to show kindness to the poor, not to oppress the orphan nor repulse the beggar) poor relief is still expressly associated with religious institutions. The mosques have been endowed with large funds for ecclesiastical and charitable purposes, one portion of which was set aside by Suleiman the Magnificent for the support of institutions such as Poor Laws provide elsewhere, including, however, baths and fountains. And the Greeks, at any rate in Constantinople, provide for the wants of their own people in a somewhat similar way, by committees of five leading members selected from the congregation of each parish church at an annual vestry meeting.

At the Reformation it became evident that the
nations which had accepted the change in religion could
no longer, for a variety of reasons, of which the splitting
up into sects and the confiscation of Church property may
be assigned as the chief, depend upon the Church for the
adequate administration of relief. This was due not so
much to the mere dissolution of the monasteries, as
Adam Smith puts it, but to the altered relations between
Church and State; and especially to the conception of a
National Church, which made it natural for the State to
prescribe, or itself to undertake, functions and duties
hitherto appropriated to the Church, regarded as an
independent body. A curious and convincing proof of
this is to be found in the fact that in Sweden, where
the connection between Church and State has always
been of the closest, the "first State law which laid the
foundation of poor relief was the Church ordinance of
1571." It is possible, moreover, that the special form
which Poor Law legislation everywhere adopted, namely,
the parochial or communal, was determined by a revival
of the old principle of local government, of which the
village community was the primitive type, being regarded
as a self-contained society capable of making fit provision
for the wants of its own members. However this may
be, there sprang up everywhere, during the earlier part of
this second period, the simplest form of Poor Laws, which
consisted in a command from the State that each parish
should in some way or other maintain its own poor, and
should appoint "overseers" to discharge the duty thus
legally imposed upon it. At Hamburg, so early as 1529,
directions were published for the guidance of the overseers; "to visit the houses in their respective districts

once every month, in order to make themselves acquainted with the circumstances of the poor; to provide employment for those who were able to work; to lend money without interest to those who were honest, and could with a little assistance maintain an independent position; and lastly, to grant permanent relief to the disabled and sick."[1] It would be difficult, with all our experience, to give a better account of the spirit which ought to preside over the administration of poor relief than this; and we may add, a similar spirit may be (though more faintly) discerned in English legislation during the reigns of the Tudor kings, previous to the definite establishment of poor relief in 1601. Two years later, in 1531, the Emperor, Charles V., directed collections to be made in all places throughout the Netherlands for the settled poor—the idlers and rogues to be set to work, poor women and children provided for; the latter put to school, and afterwards placed out in service or in trade.[2] A law of the German Empire, in 1577, compelled parishes " to support their own poor, send away strangers, and provide accommodation for the sick." And to take an instance from Scandinavian nations, the "fundamental code" of Denmark, dated 1683, formally asserted the right of needy persons to receive public assistance.

Thus there was established all over northern Europe

---

[1] The references throughout this chapter are, except when indicated, to the Reports on Poor Laws in foreign countries, published in 1875. As they can easily be found under each separate State, it has not been thought worth while to encumber our pages with special references.

[2] *Quarterly Review*, December 1835, which also quotes from the Capitularies of Charlemagne. " Suos quæque civitas alito pauperes."

an artless but thoroughly well-meaning system of poor
relief, according to which each locality was expected
to make provision for the three main classes of paupers,
the vagrant, the impotent, and the able-bodied out of
work, using upon the whole its own discretion in
furtherance of this end, subject to certain enactments
which were more of the nature of suggestions than of
positive obligation. Something of this still lingers on in
the Baltic Provinces of the Russian Empire, with the
parish committee, parish wardens, the power to set men
to work, and (what was added afterwards) magisterial or
police control.

Meanwhile, in southern Europe, during the same period,
except that in France purely ecclesiastical management
of charities had been to some extent combined with State
supervision, things went on much as they had done before
until the French Revolution. Then, and at each succeed-
ing revolutionary outbreak, attempts were made to in-
augurate a system of national compulsory relief under the
influence of the socialistic spirit; but the struggle ended
in the establishment of a form of poor relief that may
be described as organized charity with each local commune for the area of administration. Perhaps the
most impressive and final argument against legal or State
relief was the spectacle of the abuses which a continuance
of bad legislation had introduced into all the countries
where Poor Laws had taken root. To the Committee of
the National Assembly our Poor Law seemed, and with
justice, to be the "plague spot of England." But then
the French Revolution itself gave the impulse to that
series of reforming movements all over Europe which
has lasted till the present time, and produced remarkably

similar effects in various countries. This is our third or
reforming period, during which Poor Laws, among other
institutions, have been everywhere made the subject of
careful inquiry and sweeping changes, especially in respect
of the authorities to whom their administration has been
committed. Whence has arisen the state of things now
existing, which we will proceed briefly to sketch, taking
the authorities in the order of parochial (or communal),
provincial, central, and municipal.

Before doing so one preliminary distinction must be
drawn that reflects little credit upon our national reputation for common sense. Other countries found ready
made to their hands a living and useful system of local
government upon which they could and did graft the
administration of poor relief. In England alone the
humiliating truth must be confessed that no such system
was to be found, and that whatever local government we
possess at this moment has to a great extent grown up
out of our Poor Law legislation. Thus the Local Government Board of to-day is merely the old Poor Law Commission of 1834, with new duties attached to it. The
Guardians of Unions have by very slow degrees come to
have other than Poor Law functions intrusted to them ;
while, as though to emphasise our most characteristic
defects, the rate by which moneys (in rural parishes) are
raised for all local purposes is still called the Poor Rate.
What a curious chapter in the history of legislation does
this one small fact point back to !

(1.) The Parish or Commune is all over Europe recognised as the unit of Poor Law administration, though
under very different conditions. In Norway alone, where
a plan of very minute subdivision prevails, do the local

authorities appear to be in any way independent of the
parish; they consist of special commissions, with the
clergyman at their head in villages, and a magistrate in
towns.   The abuses, however, were such that in 1863
the power of levying special rates was taken from them
and given to the parish, to which they are now virtually
responsible.   In most countries the Communal Board is
also the primary Poor Law authority; this is the case in
Sweden, Denmark, Prussia, Holland, Bavaria, Austria,
and also in Italy and Portugal, where their duties in respect of poor relief are of a very minor character.   But
this arrangement is modified by the fact that in all the
more important cases the Communal Board is empowered
and expected to elect special committees, partly out of
their own number, partly such of the leading inhabitants
as are most fit to be trusted with the work, and who, as
in Prussia, are compelled to serve under a penalty.   In
France, although the commune is still the administrative
area, the separation of Poor Law duties from the commune goes a step further, "for the Legislature has separated the management of the funds destined for the poor
from that of the municipal finances; and the interests
of the poor are confided to other hands than those which
undertake the general interests of the commune."   After
much contention, it was settled in 1872 to continue the
plan of two separate (unpaid) commissions in each Commune: one to superintend the indoor relief of hospitals,
asylums, and almshouses, the other to direct the local
Board of out-relief (*Bureau de bienfaisance*), which every
commune is at liberty to establish, though until recently
two-thirds of the whole country appear to be without
them, their place in some cases being supplied by a

humbler but similar institution called the *Bureau de Charité.* These committees are, however, still connected with the communal authorities, who appoint two members, together with the mayor as *ex officio* chairman. The remaining members are nominated by very various authorities, such as the Prefect, the Court of Appeal, the Chamber of Commerce, the Bishop of the Diocese, the Presbyterian Council, and the Jewish Consistory. When appointed, they appear to be practically independent of the Commune, though not of other higher authorities.

The same system obtains in Belgium, but the Communes elect all the members of the committees and inspect their accounts, and thereby exercise a much larger control. In Saxony, on the other hand (which presents perhaps an instance of the most careful and elaborate Poor Law legislation to be found out of England), we have the opposite extreme of an almost complete separation of the Parochial from the Poor Law authorities. The plan there is, that the "Head Boroughs" of the villages (themselves nominated by the Government) shall constitute a Poor Law Board, composed of the "inhabitants of the district who are conspicuous by their intelligence, their experience, the active interest they show in all matters of public utility, and the confidence they enjoy among their fellow-citizens." It is further prescribed that landowners, clergymen, schoolmasters, presidents of private charitable institutions, and physicians, should be always invited to join the committees, and that such officials as the Head Boroughs themselves, judges, and trustees of charitable foundations, should be members *ex officio.*

The employment of assistant officers seems generally left to the discretion of the local authorities, who do not, as far as can be seen, rely much upon paid help. In France, the duties of relieving officers,—besides, of course, the work of indoor-relief,—is largely performed by members of female religious orders, who, it is said, discharge the various tasks of supervision, inquiry, and furnishing reports, with much devotion and intelligence. They receive salaries for their work. In New York State, incredible as it may sound, the overseers were—perhaps are—paid a fee for each pauper relieved. It is only necessary to add that in most countries of Northern Europe there exists a power of forming Unions of small parishes for such objects as the establishment of workhouses, or the suppression of mendicity, and, on the other hand, of dividing large districts and placing them under local sub-committees. It does not very clearly appear how far these powers are acted upon, but probably not to so great an extent as to interfere with communal authority or responsibility.

(2.) The duties of provincial authorities, are, as might be supposed, of the slightest. We may notice, however, that in some places they exercise a control over the accounts; that (*e.g.* in Prussia, where there are thirty-six provincial Unions) they relieve those who cannot be made chargeable to any special Commune; that they sometimes decide disputes between Poor Boards, especially in respect of "settlement;" and that in France the establishments for abandoned children and lunatics are departmental and not communal, as also is the Correctional Workhouse or *Dépôt de Mendicité.* The department may also, in case of necessity, subsidise the

communal treasury, and the budget of all charitable
establishments is submitted to the Prefect.

(3.) There is no special department of the Central
Government charged with the duty of managing the
administration of poor relief, except in Sweden, which
framed its laws upon the English model, and where it is
said the working people used to demand out-relief because they had been told it was given in England.
There we find a Central Board and an officer called his
Majesty's Governor. Elsewhere the State does little but
exercise such general control as a Minister of Interior
can always bring to bear upon local or provincial authorities. Sometimes the State, as in Prussia, distributes a
small sum of money on its own account, generally to the
widows and orphans of soldiers, sometimes in aid of local
Unions. In France all establishments for indoor-relief
are under State supervision, and are, of course, liable to
be interfered with by zealous ministers. But as a rule
that which constitutes the special excellence of the
English system,—control by a central authority, able to
impart something of scientific exactness into the administration of relief,—is not sought for in foreign countries,
unless it be to some extent in the United States, where
there are Central Boards, who examine and pass accounts,
can admit and transfer paupers to the various charitable
institutions, and possess certain "advisory" powers.
But it is impossible to give any adequate idea of so very
complicated a system as that which prevails in the
United States.

(4.) In respect of large cities every other nation except our own has understood—first, that they require a
different organization from that which answers in rural

or small places; secondly, that emancipation from the
control of the Town Council must lead to administrative
weakness.   Hence there is no such thing as separate
Boards of Guardians in large towns, except once more
in America, though in many places the plan has been
adopted of establishing a Board of Relief that "should
have its root in the municipality, and yet act independently of it." At Hamburg, indeed, which is the parent
of this system, the General Board for the Relief of the
Poor is only connected with the Town Council by having
representatives from it, and being presided over by a
burgomaster. In Leipzig the "Directorium" is authorized
by the Council to administer relief, and is liable to control, or even dismissal, by superior authority; in other
respects it chooses its own officers and modes of carrying
on its work.   In Paris (and Lyons) there is a special
administration, with twenty districts for outdoor-relief,
each with a council held at the *mairie*, the mayor being
president, and the whole subject to the Prefect of the
Seine.   It is, however, impossible to enter more fully
into details, though, when we come to speak of modes of
investigation, we shall have to recur to the very interesting and valuable experiments that are being carried on
in some German cities.   Suffice it to say that Committees
or Boards, connected more or less closely with the
municipalities, are everywhere the rule.

II. *The Funds from which relief is administered.*—
These may be classified as follows :—(*a*) Rates; (*b*)
Special Taxes; (*c*) Communal Property; (*d*) Endow-
ments; (*e*) Charitable Offerings; (*f*) Repayment recovered
from paupers or their friends.   These form the revenue

of the Communes, and we may complete the list by adding (*g*) Subsidies from the revenue of the State, and (*h*) of the Department.   Setting aside our own country, where the funds are raised entirely by local rates, and America, where they are paid by appropriations out of the general taxation of the towns and of the States, the invariable rule is that the necessary funds are provided by the Commune from one or more of the above-named sources (with subsidies from the State), and are made over to the Communal Committee or Poor Board to which the administration of relief is entrusted.   That is to say, the ordinary communal revenue does not (with the possible exception of Denmark) defray the cost of poor relief, which is provided for by special portions of the communal resources that have been either by law or private gifts appropriated to the relief of destitution.

We shall select as an example of the various sources from which communal poor funds are commonly derived the case of Saxony, which includes all the more important ones, and may therefore give the reader a fair idea of the state of things that prevails generally.   They are no less than fifteen in number, and may be supplemented by rates if required.

Casual Receipts. — (1.) Collections at weddings and other Church ordinances.

(2.) Taxes levied wherever there is a change in the ownership of property.

(3.) Legacies and donations.

(4.) Duties upon inheritances.

(5.) Money collected in boxes at post-offices, inns, etc. etc.·

(6.) Taxes paid for public performances, exhibitions, etc. etc.

(7.) Fines appropriated by law for poor relief.

Regular Receipts.—(8.) Collections made at churches, and gifts from Church property.

(9.) Contributions from the revenues of communities.

(10.) Voluntary house to house collections, or, in lieu of this, rates, wherever they have been declared permanent by the Poor Law Board.

(11.) Contributions of private clubs.

Other Receipts belonging to the Poor Law Fund itself.—(12). Interest and rent of property.

(13.) Paupers' work.

(14.) Repayments by paupers who have subsequently prospered.

(15.) Property left by paupers who have died in public hospitals.

How far in rural districts these sources of income require to be supplemented by the communal treasury it is impossible to say ; but if Hamburg, Berlin, and Elberfeld may be taken as fair specimens of the state of things in German towns, the supplementary grant far exceeds the original revenue. Thus at Hamburg in 1870 the private revenue was £25,783, and the grant from the public treasury was £60,453. At Berlin the grant in aid was nearly five times the amount of the Poor Fund, £136,867 to £28,650, and of this latter £8684 was recovered from paupers or their relations. At Elberfeld the two were more nearly equal, though the grant from the municipal funds was still the larger, £7424 to £5901.

We shall now select a few other characteristic or

important sources of revenue that are made use of in other countries.

In Sweden the Commune levies a special tax on manufacturers who have drawn together a large working population, and it also receives compensation from the State for relief granted to soldiers, sailors, and labourers in public employ. Norway levies a tax (communal) on cards, spirits, and beer. Sweden, again, exacts a Poll Tax upon every male over eighteen to the amount of 6½d. per annum, and upon every female to the amount of 3¼d. Saxe Coburg appropriates the profits of a gymnasium. Leipzig sends round subscription collectors armed with powers that recall the old joke, "There is no compulsion, only you must," for it is "known that those who deny themselves or refuse to contribute are liable to be summoned and taxed." Austria confiscates part of the property of Catholic clergymen who die intestate. Rome demands a contribution from newly created cardinals. Bavaria insists that workmen employed out of their own commune shall pay to a sick fund, and compels employers to make some provision for their work-people, generally by contributing to a benefit club. Charities in France derive benefits from burial-grounds, theatres, pawnshops (so also in Italy), and lotteries. The Greek Committees make a good thing out of the sale of candles; while, to crown the list, a single caged nightingale is said to pay five thalers a year to the poor fund at Elberfeld.

In Holland, we may add, the sources of public relief are almost entirely charitable, and it is only after rigorous investigation that the law allows subsidies to be made to the various charitable institutions to which the reliev-

ing of the destitute is formally made over, and which
are all more or less subject to municipal control. But
even so the tendency to rely upon public money seems
exceedingly strong, as indeed is sure to be the case.
Thus, in 1871, out of a total expenditure of £897,139,
32 per cent (£287,011) was provided from the public
revenue, of which £203,247 went to subsidise the
charities.

The evidence from France points to a similar conclusion.   There the customary municipal subsidy varies in
amount from more than one-half in the department of
the Seine (Paris) to somewhat more than one sixth in
the provinces.   If to this we add the fact that the State
or the Department maintain certain institutions for indoor-
relief (in France the State maintains seven in whole or
in part, one of them being an asylum for the blind,
founded in 1260 by St. Louis), we shall appreciate the
force of the remarks made in the report from Belgium :—
"In theory the relief of the poor is essentially a communal duty, and should cost nothing to the province or
the State.   In practice, however, both these bodies are
obliged to assume some share of the burden."   So that
the distinction between legal and charitable relief, as
practised in England and France respectively, becomes
comparatively unimportant.   Both systems have indeed
their one strong point.   In England the wholesome rule
(too much of late departed from) that localities should
defray the cost of their own poor relief tends to keep
pauperism down.   In France (and elsewhere) the organization and supervision of charity prevents a thousand evils.

III. *Those to whom relief is administered.*—The causes

and conditions of indigence are everywhere the same, and produce the same classes of pauperised persons. These need not, therefore, be separately treated, but we shall attempt to give a general view of all the various kinds of persons to whom the name Pauper has been or may be correctly applied.

There is a broad distinction made by nature itself between the impotent and the able-bodied. The first may be divided into two classes : those who have never had the chance of providing for themselves, and those who have had the chance and neglected to use it. The second also may be divided into those who are (presumably) willing to get their own living, but are prevented by adverse circumstances, and those who notoriously decline to work. Hence we have these four classes :—

First, The impotent who suffer from no fault of their own, among whom may be included (*a*) the constitutionally infirm, *e.g.* the blind ; (*b*) imbeciles of different kinds ; (*c*) fatherless children, whether orphans, deserted, or bastards.

Second, The impotent who might have done better for themselves by the exercise of virtue and forethought. These include (*d*) the aged ; (*e*) the permanently sick (*i.e.* who have become so more or less early in life) ; (*f*) lying-in women (unmarried).

Thirdly, The able-bodied who, as being settled in one place, and having some ostensible means of gaining a living, are nevertheless out of work. Under this head may be included paupers (*g*) from lack of employment, (*h*) from temporary illness, (*i*) from insufficient wages to support the families dependent on them.

Fourthly, The able-bodied who notoriously prefer idle

ness to work, and who may be divided into (*j*) mendicants and (*k*) vagrants.

To these eleven classes we may add a twelfth, namely
—(*l*) Widows with families, whom, though "able-bodied"
themselves, they cannot nevertheless be expected to
maintain, even with full employment. These form everywhere the recipients of poor relief called paupers, and a
mere glance at the list will serve to show how varied are
the problems which Poor Law administration is expected
to grapple with, and how likely it is that mistakes should
be made.

IV. *The Methods by which relief is administered.*—
These once more are the same in all places, and are too
familiar to need explanation. They are divided into two
kinds, corresponding broadly with the two classes of
impotent and able-bodied, as above described; that is to
say, indoor-relief as generally employed for the former,
and out-relief for the latter,—vagrants, however, being
exceptionally dealt with. Of these we may also enumerate twelve principal ones, as follows :—

Indoor-relief, comprising (*a*) poorhouses (this general
term includes almshouses and workhouses, which practically are not distinguishable); (*b*) hospitals ; (*c*) asylums :
(*d*) schools, including reformatories ; (*e*) vagrant wards.

Out-relief, comprising (*f*) gifts of money ; (*g*) gifts in
kind ; (*h*) giving of employment ; (*i*) apprenticing of
children ; (*j*) medical attendance ; (*k*) burial.

To these may be added, as something that partakes
of the nature of both out and indoor relief, and is perhaps older than either, the curious plan of (*l*) boarding
out which still survives in some places. Of this (the rest

speak for themselves) a brief explanation may not be uninteresting, especially as we shall come upon some trace of it in the "Roundsman" of the old English Poor Law. It was found convenient in early times, and in thinly-populated agricultural districts, to lodge the paupers out,—that is, to place them with householders in rotation, to be fed and sheltered. This custom, which was once widely extended, and still lingers on in parts of Austria and Sweden, is in full operation in Norway alone, where it is called the "Lægd." In 1832 very minute regulations were issued to prevent abuses, the superintendent of the lægd being required to report improper conduct on either side, and have the parties fined or imprisoned. The peasants to this day uphold the system, believing that it takes no more to feed an extra guest, and that to receive him keeps alive the feeling of voluntary benevolence. But the farmers, who are liable to have whole families quartered upon them for relief, either in their own houses or at the paupers' home, make many complaints of indolent and impertinent guests.

The reader will not expect any account of the multitudinous varieties of operation by which the above-mentioned (12) methods are applied to the relief of the (12) classes of indigent persons covered by the name pauper : there is the less occasion for this, inasmuch as, compared with the general resemblance, the differences are but superficial. Practically, whether by State-guaranteed support, or by organized and subsidised charity, or by a mere abundance of voluntary benevolence (as in Italy and Portugal), there are established all over Europe local authorities to whom the pauper can apply in expectation of receiving that sort of relief which is deemed suitable to his case, and which, we strongly suspect, differs very little indeed in different countries. On the other hand, the absence of those two main points of the English system, central control and the workhouse test, does certainly produce some results which it is well worth our while to point out.

First, we may notice that there is a unanimous complaint on the part of all English inquirers that foreign countries fall far below our own in the important particular of obtaining trustworthy statistics; Sweden, which possesses a central Department, being the only exception. Thus, of France it is said that "statistics are collected somewhat irregularly;" of Belgium, that "there are no published Poor Law returns for the whole kingdom since 1858;" of Prussia, that "the absence of statistical information in a country where social subjects are so closely studied is attributed to the fact that each commune would start from a more or less different basis;" of the United States, "that a sound basis for calculating the comparative amount of pauperism in England and America is altogether wanting," Massachusetts, however, forming a partial exception.

From the absence of local control it follows that the communal authorities,—that is, the Poor Law Board, which represents them,—possess a discretion as to the administration of relief far beyond that enjoyed by an English Board of Guardians. The State contents itself with, at most, laying down certain principles, and then leaving it to the Poor Law Boards to carry them out in their own way; even in Sweden the Poor Law Boards determine independently the manner of relief, which may, according to the law, "vary with the peculiarities of the dis-

trict." In Saxony "the State interferes only in cases
of necessity." Generally speaking, the rule is that the
State insists upon the commune providing relief for the
destitute, defines who the destitute are, and then leaves
it to the discretion of the local authorities. Of this rule
the Prussian law of 1871 may serve as an example :—
"Every German has, in case of distress, the right to
demand of his commune a roof, the absolute necessaries
of life, medical attendance in case of illness, and in case
of death a suitable burial. Relief may be granted either
by admission into a poorhouse or hospital, or by allotting
work proportioned to the strength of the pauper, either
in such an institution or out of it."

The conditions of indoor-relief are also in some respects different from what they are in England, owing
to the absence of the Workhouse Test. In foreign
countries the functions of an English workhouse are
divided between almshouses where relief is administered,
and correctional houses where repression is carried on to
an extent unknown amongst ourselves. These last belong
to our next division, and will be mentioned hereafter.
As to the almshouses, the inmates are much the same as
in an English workhouse, namely, the aged, infirm, and
sick ; the number of children, it is to be hoped, is growing less. But, as the poorhouse is not used as a test of
want, the need of repressive discipline is not felt ; and
the natural sentiments of compassion towards the kind
of persons who occupy it tend to make it a tolerably easy
and even indulgent place of residence. Complaints upon
this head are constant. Thus, to take two instances, the
workhouse in Copenhagen was said some ten years ago
to be an example of all that such an institution should

not be. Brandy to the amount of 6000 quarts, and
tobacco to the amount of 1000 dollars, were sold every
year to the inmates, of whom in 1867 about half absconded
with property belonging to the house.   At Elberfeld the
poorhouse, though not very well arranged, is occupied
by a contented set of inmates, who are well fed and clad,
and enjoy their freedom,—those who can work going out
by day to do it, and receiving for their own use whatever
they earn above the cost of their maintenance.   "In
short" (as the report says) "an old Elberfeld pauper
smoking his eternal pipe in the day-room of the poorhouse may well feel that he has got a comfortable asylum
for the close of his days."   We may notice that the almshouse or asylum for the aged and infirm is an important
institution in America, where also it was liable to many
of the worst abuses of the old English poorhouse; but
these have been of late years reformed by sending the
able-bodied paupers, tramps, and others, who used to
throng to them in winter or when suffering from disease,
to houses of correction.   In America the adaptation of
houses to the different classes of paupers seems excel-
lently done.

It may be mentioned here that the practice of exact-
ing from indoor paupers remunerative labour either at
their own trades or at some occupation suitable to their
capacity, still prevails on the Continent,—at any rate
among the northern nations.   Public opinion in England
has clearly pronounced this to be an economical and also
a Poor Law mistake.   But this general rule does not apply
to task-work done at houses of correction.

As to out-relief in foreign countries, it would seem to
be, as might be expected, upon the whole much more

capricious and unequal, much more unsatisfactory, and, in proportion to its amount, more pauperising, than in England, where in truth there is not much to boast of. It is kept down certainly in France, and probably elsewhere, by the fact that it is limited not by the extent of destitution to be relieved, but by the amount of the funds which the authorities have to spend. But then this leads to a system of small temporary doles that pauperise without relieving. Then again, the Bureaus are said to be too numerous and badly arranged. Then again, there are the usual complaints that the administration of relief is confided to overseers, often small shopkeepers, who have no time to obtain the necessary information, and, being afraid of incurring odium, "fall into habits of blind and wholesale benevolence." And lastly, there is a growing conviction that in every case the amount of pauperism depends not upon the circumstances of the working classes, but upon the facility with which help may be obtained. The crucial instance is Belgium, where the communes possessed of the largest charitable resources have the most paupers, and Luxembourg, with next to no revenues, has also next to no pauperism.

It may serve to illustrate the confusion and uncertainty still prevalent upon this subject, that in America the State of New York, on the one hand (taught by the disastrous results of indiscriminate charity), in 1876 resolved to make no appropriation of funds for out-relief, and that the State of Massachusetts in the same year passed an Act for the express purpose of extending it.

V. *Repressive Measures.* — We shall take the means whereby legislators have endeavoured to prevent the abuses of poor relief in their chronological order, and arrange them as follows :—

(*a*) Punishment, or the simple remedy of earlier times, now confined to vagrants, impostors, and incorrigibles.

(*b*) Settlement, or the first limitation of the conditions upon which relief was given, *i.e.* that a pauper had only a claim for relief upon his own parish.

(*c*) Compulsory maintenance, including payments by friends, and repayments by the pauper himself.

Direct repression, including (*d*) house test; (*e*) labour test; (*f*) correctional houses; (*g*) criminal punishment; and (*h*) investigation, this latter being used not only as a means of discovery, but as a repelling measure. These methods of direct repression form the modern solution of the pauper difficulty, and touch by far the hardest and most debated problems of poor relief.

The broad distinction between the English method of applying repression (which, of course, we shall consider at length in its place) and the foreign may be summed up in one short but important proposition. In England every other mode of repression is much less stringent than elsewhere, because the workhouse test has superseded them all. With us the relieving authority can offer the House, whenever there is any uncertainty as to the reality of the destitution, and the result naturally follows that, having this formidable and efficient weapon to fall back on, punitive regulations even in the case of "tramps" are almost unknown; settlement is becoming quite a simple and easy matter; the distinction between relief in money and in kind, which is much thought of on the Continent, is practically neglected; maintenance by friends is not half enough insisted on; and investigation, as elsewhere understood, there is far too little. Leaving this, however, for its proper place, we go on to give some account of the principle of repressive measures as carried out all over the world.

(1.) Punishment was the only remedy provided against pauperism (then known only under the forms of begging, whether by mendicants or vagrants) during all those long centuries when punishment was least deserved by the pauper, and might, from our present point of view, with much more reason have been inflicted on the inflictors. Pauperism was to a great extent caused, and certainly aggravated, by legislation either economically vicious, or else directed avowedly against the interests of the working classes in a spirit that can only be excused by the fact that it marked the period of transition from slavery to independence. Then it was sought to extirpate it by means that "makes this part of (English) history look like the history of savages in America. Almost all severities have been inflicted, except scalping." In England, France, Spain, and the German Empire, we read the same dismal tale of whipping, branding, the pillory, burning the ear, cropping the ear, couples chained together to cleanse sewers, long terms of imprisonment, and, finally, death itself, in hundreds every year in every country. A good deal of this severity still remains in the treatment of vagrants even now. In France Napoleon decreed that vagrancy should cease, but, as a French writer remarks, "the beggars made a mock of him who made a mock at kings. He is gone—they remain." (It is a tempting epigram to say that if in France the vagrant mastered the conqueror of kings, in England the pauper proved too much for the conqueror

of the conqueror, during whose pre-eminence in politics
nothing was done to abate the evil.) And, generally, it
may be said of all countries except our own that police
regulations of a character so harsh as to tend to defeat
their own purpose is the method adopted for dealing
with beggars, the old plan of sending them back to their
own parishes after imprisonment still finding favour.
Two exceptions, however, are noteworthy. In Italy
(the history of which is full of quaint stories of beggar
companies and their rights and customs) the infirm even
now,—that is, by a law of 1865,—receive a license to beg
upon condition of being civil, and not disgusting people
by the exhibition of their sores, thereby carrying the
mind back to the old Scotch days of that prince of
mendicants, the King's Bedesman, Edie Ochiltree by
name. And in Poland there are no restrictions at all
upon professional mendicancy, owing, it is said, to the
old Sclave superstition that it is unlucky to turn a
beggar away. Does this same superstition, it might be
asked, at all account for the persistency with which
beggars are relieved by persons much poorer than themselves in English country places?

(2.) Settlement. The meaning of this innocent-look-
ing word, big with legal intricacies and manifold disaster
to the interests of the working people, is merely that
paupers must be relieved in the place in which they are
"settled," or have "gained a settlement," and that if
they are relieved in any other parish than their own
they must be sent back to it, and the expenses of their
maintenance charged upon it. The place of settlement
or domicile, as it is called abroad, is primarily the place
where a man is born. No doubt the law of settlement

was not at first intended as a means of repression.
The Reformation was marked in some respects by a
return to the old primitive notion of village government,
and it seems to have been thought that each parish was
an independent community, capable of maintaining its
own indigents.   But as society advanced, and men,
hitherto chained to their own parishes, began to move
about in the world, a second principle,—the principle, as
it may be called, of universal selfishness, by which every
other nation, class, city, or even village, is regarded as
a kind of rival, if not enemy, against which "protective"
measures have to be taken,—began to come into operation.
The larger and wealthier parishes, on the one hand, the
landowners on the other, reaped the advantage of the
labour of workpeople, and then devised the law of settlement as an excuse for passing them back to their own
parishes in age or sickness.   In Germany the evil was
aggravated to an intolerable extent by the jealousies of
the small States, and was not finally grappled with till
the establishment of the German Empire some ten or
eleven years ago.

But whatever its origin, settlement was always practically a repressive measure.   It went upon the simple
principle that each locality knew most about its own
paupers, and could deal best with them, and it fixed the
penalty of confinement to the place of settlement upon
the pauper's head.   Hence, as less artless measures of
repression have prevailed, and a sense has grown up
that the interests of localities are after all identical, the
law of settlement has become far more lenient and
simple.   A few instances of the present state of the law
may be useful.   In France the Bureau of out-relief (or

out-charity as it might be called) may not relieve, except
the recipient has been domiciled in the commune at least
one year.   In Belgium the term of residence was first
one year, then four, then eight, and finally it was proposed, in the interests of the rural communes, to diminish
it to one.   In the German Empire, where the laws of
the separate States prescribed different periods, a Federal
law of 1870 prescribed two years as sufficient to obtain
a settlement.   In Sweden a person's settlement is in the
Union where he was last registered for Poll Tax, which
would seem practically to abolish it.   But in Holland
alone has settlement been formally done away, and
the task of relief been "committed to the humanity of
the whole nation in its different localities."   But then
Holland relies so entirely, in theory at any rate, upon the
charities, that the abolition of settlement is rendered all
the easier.

On the other hand, the State of Massachusetts in
1874 increased the already numerous ways of obtaining
settlement (resembling what will meet us in English
Poor Law history), with the intention of increasing the
proportion of outdoor to indoor relief,—a curious retro-
cession, due, we suspect, to the prevalence of American
sentiment in a sphere where sentiment has wrought
infinite harm to the very persons it meant to benefit.

(3.) Maintenance by friends and repayment by the
pauper himself form a just and obvious mode of repression, to which recourse is had universally.   Here once
more we give a few leading instances.   The duty of
maintenance in some cases (Sweden and Denmark) does
not extend beyond parents and children; and in the
latter country it would appear that the maintenance of

children is confined to eighteen years of age, and of parents to cases of disordered intellect. In France and Germany the duty ascends in the direct line, and is extended to children-in-law; in Italy brothers and sisters are included, and (apparently) by local regulations in some places in Germany, *e.g.* Berlin. In America the ordinary rule of direct ascent and descent prevails, but is "not well enforced, because of the vexation, expense, and disagreeable duty of enforcing it" (Massachusetts Report, p. 86). In Saxony even distant relations "may be invited by the Poor Law Board, in an appropriate manner, to fulfil the moral duties incumbent upon them in this respect." But what is the effect of this moral suasion does not appear.

As to repayment, great and laudable stress is laid upon this wholesome discipline in many countries. Thus, in Sweden the Poor Law Board has the right of mastership over the pauper until he has repaid the sum expended on his behalf. In Denmark the pauper's effects are registered, so as to prevent him pawning or selling his property, and the Commune has even some claim against his heir; in any case, relief is regarded as a debt to be paid even before rent or service, should his circumstances improve. The same holds in Germany, where the Commune inherits the pauper's property, and where considerable sums are retained as repayments. Thus the Commune often comes into possession of articles of furniture (sharing it with widows and children), which it sometimes lends out to deserving persons. In 1870 Berlin inherited £437 from this source.

(4.) Direct repression. Even if experience had not settled the matter, it might have been taken for certain

that, sooner or later, the need would arise for stronger and
more direct measures of repression when once an inducement had been held out to idle and worthless persons to
avail themselves of the public bounty.   And as a matter of
fact nearly every nation has had occasion to reform its
Poor Laws during the last half-century in this direction.
That is to say, there has been a recurrence to some sort
of penal legislation, in order to carry out the great principle of repression, which no one disputes in words, that
the condition of the pauper should be less favourable
than that of the self-supporting labourer.   The English
solution of the problem, namely, the imposition of the
workhouse test, has found no favour with foreign Legis-
latures, though strongly recommended by high authorities.
The reasons are partly sentimental, partly moral.   The
first is the familiar argument that it is wrong to disturb
family ties, a doctrine which in France is pushed to the
extreme of relieving the sick at home in preference to
sending them to hospitals.   Upon the same ground the
workhouse at Leipzig was finally closed in 1849, after
the experiment had been twice tried.   The American
argument is much the same, with the cry of economy
superadded.   Thus the Boston overseers declare that
"this plan would separate families, permanently pauperise them, and is a doubtful measure of humanity or
economy, as a little relief occasionally in many cases is
all that is required, and is not necessarily demoralising."
(This last clause would seem to most English authorities
fatally erroneous.)   But these arguments do not satisfy
the more advanced and thorough German thinking
which is summed up in a report on the Elberfeld system
by L. F. Seyffardt, printed in the Reports from foreign

countries. There the "moral development of the individual," "who positively deteriorates under the workhouse system," is the argument relied on, the sentimental
arguments coming second. The writer does not appear
to have a very practical knowledge of the working of
the English system, for he fails to notice that as a
matter of fact the test is so effective that few persons
who would be thought worthy of out-relief, still fewer
who would deteriorate in the workhouse, ever find their
way within its walls,—at any rate, with the intention of
remaining there for any length of time.

But the point of interest is to observe how other
countries have met the difficulty. They begin by draw-
ing a broad distinction between ordinary distress and
destitution due to the pauper's own fault, and then
proceed to visit the latter with a correctional discipline
the like to which is quite unknown amongst ourselves.
And no doubt, granting that it is within the province
and the capacity of the State to take cognisance of
degrees of moral turpitude, it is refreshing to hear of
correctional workhouses to which applicants of bad
character are forthwith consigned and made to work.
We have alluded to these before in connection with the
punishment of vagrants, but it is by no means confined
to this class of paupers. Thus in Berlin the police can
order drunkards to be confined there for any period from
one day to two years; so also in Sweden, Denmark,
Bavaria, and Baden, where idleness and prostitution are
added to the list of punishable offences; while at Elberfeld itself imprisonment for play, drink, idleness, and
even the loss of means of support, was only abolished a
few years ago against the will of the Poor Law adminis-

E

trators. In France, on the contrary, the *Dépôts de Mendicité* appear to be confined to the punishment of the vagrants or beggars for whom they were established. But the plan of correctional houses appears to have reached its greatest development in America. In New York, by a refinement of American humour, an able-bodied person applying for relief is obliged to endorse an order for admission to a workhouse for a definite period, thereby accomplishing the in other respects not very difficult task of "committing himself," and, when there, is set to some repulsive form of labour. And in Massachusetts, under an Act known as the Pipers and Fiddlers' Act, not merely rogues and vagabonds but (amongst others) stubborn children, common drunkards, night-walkers, brawlers, persons who neglect their families, frequenters of taverns and gaming-houses, and common pipers and fiddlers, may be, upon conviction, committed to the house of correction. At one time ordinary paupers were inmates of the same house, but there are now separate establishments.

There remains the larger class of paupers, whose faults, whatever they may be, do not amount to punish-able crime. For these the only alternative mode of repression is to make things very uncomfortable for them by strict investigation and close supervision. This is the secret of the celebrated system in vogue at Elberfeld and other German cities, which the author above quoted expressly describes as a substitution for the workhouse test. At Elberfeld, a town of 71,000 population, there are 18 overseers and 252 visitors, one overseer with 14 visitors having charge over each section into which the town is divided, which makes one officer to about every

260 inhabitants. The visitors meet in their sections
once a fortnight (the overseer presiding) to report and
decide on applications for relief, the conditions of obtaining which are, that the applicant (if able-bodied) should
be out of work, should be able to show that he has tried
to obtain it, and should be willing to do what work is
found for him. But before obtaining it he must answer
every question in a "Question Paper," which really
seems in our English eyes a kind of instrument of mental
torture. It begins (at Leipzig, where there is the same
system) with a little homily upon the necessity of can-
dour, obedience, and modesty, and upon the results of
pauperism to the recipient. He must give information
as to every detail of his life, e.g. his work, change of
residence, property, furniture. He must not keep a dog,
nor go to a place of public entertainment. He is
"constantly," i.e. not less than once a fortnight, looked
up by the visitor, and every change is noted and reported. He must declare whether his family leads a
moral and honest life, and "specify which members do
not." The visitor is expected to reprimand disorderly
conduct, to enforce cleanliness and honesty, to warn
parents of their duties—especially education—towards
their children, and children of theirs—especially rever-
ence—towards their parents. In short, he must "strive
to exercise a healthy influence over the moral feelings of
the poor."

There can be no doubt as to the efficiency of this
system of investigation as a repressive measure. In 1852
the number of paupers at Elberfeld was estimated at
4000 in a population of 50,000, or about 1 in 12. In
1873 it was 1863 in a population of 71,000, or about 1

in 38.   But it is somewhat ominous that, as in the case
of our own country, a reaction set in, and there were in
1873 800 more paupers than in 1869; the increase in
population is, however, not stated for any year later than
1869, and the growth of pauperism is in part set down
to the late Franco-German war.   But, under any circumstances, the results are much the same as in the best
English Unions.

VI. *Remedial Measures.* — Upon these we do not
propose to speak at length.   Some of them, such as
moral supervision, procuring (private) employment, have
been touched upon already, though the appointment of
trustees in Saxony for drunkards and extravagant persons, to prevent them becoming chargeable, deserves a
special word of mention.   Others, such as loans, migra-
tion, emigration, allotments (more than 2000 persons
rent potato ground of the Commune in Berlin, upon the
recommendation of the Poor Law Board), do not need
explanation.   Others, such as sanitary inspection, school
attendance, and vaccination, are only accidentally united
with poor relief administration.   But the truth is, that
although the raising of the working classes above the
need of pauperism is in theory set forth as one, if not
the principal, object of legislation, yet what was said of
the New York Society for Improving the Condition of
the Poor applies in all cases :—" Its design is stated to
be 'the elevation of the physical and moral condition of
the indigent, and, so far as is compatible with these
objects, the relief of their necessities.' *In practice its
operations are confined to the giving of relief."*
But the trial of remedial measures is perhaps yet to

come, and meanwhile the bare statement of such aims testifies to a growing desire to promote the welfare of labour. And though Burke's dictum is unquestionably true, that it is "not in the power of Governments to do much positive good," yet they can and ought to remove the evils which the ignorance or selfishness of previous generations have allowed to grow up. And especially something can be done to put the relations of charity and State relief upon a sounder footing. As a specimen of what has been attempted, and of what may be hoped for hereafter, we may fittingly bring this chapter to a close with the mention of the plan which the city of Boston adopted some years ago. The Corporation built, at a cost of 200,000 dollars, a Bureau of relief, at which, besides the offices for the overseers, there were also offices set apart for various charitable organisations, a registration of charities, and temporary homes for women and children. Applicants are referred then and there to the particular charity which can deal with their case, and thus some progress is made in what must be pronounced the capital article of future administration of relief,— namely, the separation between cases which can be dealt with by the public authorities without doing more harm to the community than they do good to the individual, and those which require the patience, the painstaking, and the benevolent sympathy that can be looked for from charity, and from charity alone.

CHAPTER III.

POOR LAW HISTORY.[1]

THE existing system of poor relief in England is so entirely, both as to its principles and its institutions, a matter of gradual growth, that in giving some account of the earlier Poor Law we shall be virtually describing the essential elements and main features of that which is at present established. And as the history, even in the brief compendium which is all that we can attempt, is both interesting and valuable, whereas the details of administration can with difficulty be made so, we are the less reluctant to beg the reader's attention to what is, in truth, a singular episode in the annals of our social progress.

The old Poor Law came to an end, as most people know, in 1834; previous to which time it may be divided into three distinctly marked periods.

[1] The authorities for the next two chapters are mainly—Nicholls's *History of the English Poor Law;* the Report of the Poor Law Commissioners in 1834 ; the Sixth Report of the Poor Law Commission in 1839 ; an article in the *Edinburgh Review,* Number 149, on Poor Law Reform, attributed to Mr. Nassau Senior ; and an article in the *Quarterly Review,* Number 106, attributed to Sir Francis Head, on English Charity. Reference has been made to the original standard work on the subject—Sir Frederick Eden's *State of the Poor,* published in 1797.

First, down to the death of Elizabeth in 1603, or more strictly to the famous Act which definitely established poor relief in England in 1601.

Second, down to a somewhat uncertain date, for which the accession of George III. in 1760 may be taken as a convenient point.

Third, down to the Reform of 1834.

The First Period.—Down to the reign of Elizabeth it cannot be said that Poor Laws, in our sense of the word (*i.e.* measures for the relief of destitution), existed at all; they might more fittingly be called laws against the poor and the rights of labour. The attempt was made persistently for 250 years, so far as the passing of repressive and penal laws could accomplish it, to reduce the labourer to the state of servitude from which it is but fair to remember he was but just emerging. To carry out this object he was confined to his place of birth; he was compelled to work for wages fixed, sometimes by law (*e.g.* that he should accept the current wages of the last five or six years), sometimes by justices, themselves employers of labour, every half-year according to the price of provisions; and if, from any vague idea of bettering his condition, he wandered abroad in search of work at the highest attainable price, he rendered himself liable to barbarous punishments (mentioned in the last chapter), which there is some reason for believing were not very commonly inflicted. At any rate, each successive Act testified to the failure of the attempt, "notwithstanding the good statutes before made," and we may therefore content ourselves with one illustration of the spirit that governed the whole series. The Act of Henry IV.,

passed in 1405, recites that the law preventing the removal of labourers into large towns was evaded by the
practice of apprenticing quite young children to divers
crafts within cities and boroughs, "so that there is so
great scarcity of labourers and other servants of hus-
bandry that the GENTLEMEN and other people of the
realm be greatly impoverished;" which practice it then
proceeds to forbid (except the parent have property in
the borough), upon pain of forfeiture of the indentures,
of one year's imprisonment, and of fine levied upon the
parent at the king's pleasure, and upon the employer to
the amount of one hundred shillings.

As is commonly the case, things were at the darkest
before the dawn.   At no time were the vagrancy laws
more severe or more severely administered than in the
reign of Henry VIII., when, as the modern undergraduate
may like to know, his predecessors swelled the number
of "valiant rogues," under the title of "Oxford and
Cambridge scholars that go about begging."   But during
this time of social dislocation and religious strife the
labourer did but share the fate which befell all that was
best and worthiest in the nation.   It is more pleasant
and not less profitable to observe that the tide of amendment was already setting strongly in, and that the
struggle between the old and the new spirit, which was
nowhere more clearly marked than in the treatment of
the indigent, was ended by the victory of the latter,
sooner perhaps in England than in other countries.   The
older spirit was still represented by the enactment of the
old ferocious laws against "sturdy vagabonds;" but so
early as 1536 the first distinction was drawn between
"poor impotent, sick, and diseased people, not being able

to work, who may be provided for, holpen, and relieved,"
and "such as be lusty, who, having their limbs strong
enough to labour, may be daily kept in continual labour,
whereby every one of them may get their own living
with their own hands." To carry out the first object
the clergy were to exhort the people to charitable offerings, and were to keep a book to show how the money
raised was expended. The idea thus started spread
rapidly. In 1551 it was enacted that in order to provide
for the "impotent, feeble, and lame, WHO ARE POOR IN
VERY DEED," collectors of alms at church on Sundays
should be appointed; that, in case of refusal, the Bishop
is to send for the recusant to expostulate with him, and—
by a later Act—should bind him over to appear before
the Justices, who, after "charitably and gently persuading
him," should themselves levy a tax upon him at their
discretion. But it is satisfactory to think that all throughout the reign of Elizabeth the "poor in very deed" felt
more and more the effects of that growing spirit of *humanity* which was distilled from that splendid company of
men who gathered round her throne. A register of impotent folk was to be kept, and a convenient dwelling-
place found for them; officers, under the name of collectors, overseers, governors, censors, wardens, were appointed to relieve them; provision was made for maintenance by relations, the case of illegitimate children
being expressly included; houses of correction were
ordered to be built, and "stuff" for work provided. So
that the definite establishment of a system of poor relief
in 1601 was only the completion of previous measures
by the addition of a compulsory rating instead of voluntary or quasi-voluntary contributions. And it is, we

think, clear beyond reasonable doubt that it was the growing sense of what the nation owed to itself, the mere consideration of natural humanity and collective responsibility, that was the immediate and efficient cause of the institution of Poor Laws, as we now understand them.

The Second Period.—The Act of 1601, the "foundation and text-book of English Poor Law," dealt with the authorities, the funds, the recipients, and the methods of poor relief. As to the first of these, it was ordered that two or three overseers were to be nominated in every parish in Easter week, under the hand and seal of Justices of the Peace, and were to take order with consent of the justices for carrying out the Act. As to funds they were to raise weekly or otherwise such sums of money as they thought fit by taxation of every inhabitant, the parson heading the list—a post of honour and of burden which, owing to the nature of his income, he occupies to this day. In the case of poor parishes a rate in aid to be levied upon the Hundred or county was permitted, but not, it should seem, acted upon in practice. As to the recipients and methods of relief, a distinction was drawn between children whose parents could not keep them, persons able to work but without occupation, and the impotent, *e.g.* the lame, old, and blind— the first were to be apprenticed, the second set to work ("stock" *e.g.* of flax being provided by the overseers), the third relieved. As to repression, liability to maintain was extended to grandparents, and it was taken for granted that a person's right to relief would arise in his birthplace.

The wisdom of the Act is almost as remarkable for what it omitted as for what it prescribed. It took notice of the only two classes who come legitimately within the province of Poor Laws,—the idle who will not, and the impotent who cannot, work; and with these it dealt by methods simple indeed and vague, but essentially true in principle. The "industrious poor," as Sir Matthew Hale expressly noticed, were not, and were never intended to be (as they never ought to be) included within its scope; while vagabonds were left to the criminal law, the labour test being adopted for persons resident in their parish and able to work if they pleased: it was only in case of refusal to work that this class was to be committed to prison. One hundred years afterwards, in 1696, a preamble of an Act in the reign of William III. shows how clearly the statesmen of that time understood the meaning of the Act to be as we have stated it: "That the money raised only for the relief of such as are as well impotent as poor may not be misapplied and consumed by idle, sturdy, and disorderly beggars." And so long as the principle of this Act was adhered to, which, with one lamentable exception, was the case for one hundred and sixty years, the working of the Poor Laws was fairly successful.

We shall give three instances of the chief alterations which were made during this period. The first concerns the authorities by whom relief was to be administered. In 1691 an Act recites that overseers, upon frivolous pretences, but chiefly for their own private ends, gave relief to what persons and number they think fit, by which means the rates are daily increased, contrary to the true intent of the Statute of the 43d of Elizabeth

The remedy provided was the very sensible one that a
register should be kept of paupers with the amount of
the relief given them ; that this register should be produced once a year at a vestry meeting; that the cases
should be examined into, and a new list made out for the
ensuing year as the parishioners shall allow ; and that no
one else during that year should "receive collection"
(*i.e.* relief) except by *authority* of one Justice, or by
order of the Bench of Justices at Quarter Sessions.

From this last clause, or rather from the perversion
of its plain meaning, sprang "all our woes." For it
appears from an Act of George I., some thirty years later,
that a practice had sprung up of Justices ordering relief
to any applicants who came to them without the knowledge of the parish officers, or upon false or frivolous
pretences, "whereby they have obtained relief" (this
phrase is characteristic ; the blame was not, as in the case
of the overseers, attached to the giver, for in those days
Justices could do no wrong), "which hath greatly contributed to the increase of the rates." Unfortunately the
usurpation was not promptly stopped, but it was merely
ordered that the applicant should be required to show
that he had first of all applied for relief to the parish
authorities, who should then be summoned to show cause
why relief should not be given. Hence, in the words of the
Report of 1834, which lays the blame of most of the harm
that followed upon this perversion of the law, "The Act
which was passed to remedy this abuse" (*i.e.* of the
Justices' interference) enabled the Justice, on the pauper's
statement of some matter which the Justice should judge
to be a cause for relief, to summon the overseers to show
cause why relief should not be given, and to order such

relief as *he* should think fit—an order against which there was no appeal." The results of this enactment we shall see presently.

The second point concerns the important article of indoor-relief, and that, too, as a test of destitution. Owing to the increase of expenditure the idea of building houses for the reception of paupers became popular, though it was mixed with the notion, so plausible in itself, but so wrong in principle and disastrous in effects, that the paupers could be put to remunerative labour. In 1696 John Locke had suggested the establishment of working schools, and the provision of materials for the employment of labourers at the public cost. Next year, at the instance of a Mr. John Carey, a workhouse was built at Bristol by special Act of Parliament, and being used as a test of destitution produced in a short time such excellent results that the example was followed by Worcester, Hull, Norwich, and other places. And in the Act of George I. above mentioned it was enacted that parishes might either singly, or in unions of two or more, provide houses for the reception of the indigent, and that "NO POOR WHO REFUSED TO BE LODGED AND KEPT IN SUCH HOUSES SHOULD BE ENTITLED TO ASK OR RECEIVE PAROCHIAL RELIEF." The immediate effect of this measure was, as might have been expected, satisfactory. The expenditure which was estimated (perhaps too highly) in 1698 at £819,000 was returned in 1750 at £619,000 in spite of the increase of population. But after the zeal of the first founders had passed away, and the evils incident to a system of management without central supervision had crept in, the tide of evil soon set in again, and in the next period in 1776 the expenditure was £1,521,000, and in 1785, upon an average of three years, the enormous sum of £1,912,000.

Upon the whole, however, it must be said that during the second period, *i.e.* down to 1760, the working of the Poor Laws was fairly successful. It is true the expenditure was increasing, just as it did in our own time some twelve years ago, but it had been partially met, as it was by ourselves, by increasing the rigour of the workhouse test. And it is to be noted that the reign of George II. is fixed upon by the best authorities as the time when the condition of the working classes was more prosperous than it had been before or has been since—until comparatively recent days. On the other hand, the germs of future evil had been already sown, and were further aggravated by the third change in the law which we are next to indicate.[1]

This third point concerns the law of settlement which,—not, however, by any effect of the Act of Elizabeth,—was made during this period intolerably harsh and oppressive. Philosophy knows how to make excuses for mistakes, or even for what appears to us wickedness, when it grows out of the spirit of the age in its advance

---

[1] The favourable opinion above expressed is borne out, *valeat quantum*, by an examination of the accounts of my own parish of Islip. These are contained in one book, dating from the year 1713 to 1781, and are arranged every year upon the same plan. Taking the year 1760 as a specimen, I find that the accounts extend over ten pages of a very large book, and are divided into the weekly pay of such impotent folk as would receive relief now, and "extra ordinaries," the latter being made up of doles to sick persons, payment of rent, molecatching (? "moldkeln" £1 : 3s.), birdminding, "anafterdavy" (? affidavit), burial, and official journeys, etc. The weekly relief was about £46, the extraordinaries £22 ; total for the year, £68 : 9 : 6. Twenty years before the amount of relief was

towards a better state ; but philosophy is thrown away
upon such a reign as that of the second Charles, the
wickedness of which was due to a deliberate reaction
against all that had been best and worthiest in preceding
reigns.   In the sphere of Poor Laws another and not
unsuccessful attempt was made to reduce the working
classes to practical servitude.   By an Act of 1662, itself
a confused and illogical medley, it was enacted at the instance chiefly of the members for London and Westminster, that at the complaint of the overseers the Justices
might, within forty days of any person's coming to dwell
in a strange parish, order him to be removed back to his
own place of settlement, unless he could give security to
the new parish against becoming chargeable to it,—that
is to say, persons could be removed not merely when they
were chargeable, but upon the chance that they might
become so.   The reason for this almost incredible viola-
tion of the rights of liberty was, that "poor people are
not restrained from going from one parish to another,
and therefore do endeavour to settle themselves in those
parishes where there is the best stock," etc. etc.   By this
Act it may with truth be said that the iron of slavery
entered into the soul of the English labourer, and made

only £37 : 0 : 10, and twenty years afterwards it had reached the
sum of £142 : 10 : 1, payments for labour having become much more
common.   The accounts are always passed by some half-dozen
parishioners, and signed as "allowed" by two Justices.   I may perhaps be permitted, under shelter of a note, to express my firm conviction that this old system of management, plus a workhouse for
each locality, supported by the county rates and used as a test,
plus also a prohibition to give out-relief to the able-bodied, and
subjected to strict supervision and audit, would be at this moment,
IN COUNTRY PLACES, a better and more effective administration
than the present one, necessary as that had become in 1834.

him cling to his parish as a shipwrecked sailor to his
raft.   From the very first it was the fruitful parent of
fraud, injustice, lavish expenditure, ill-will, and endless
litigation.   So early as 1685 an Act of James II. recites
" that poor people at their first coming into a parish do
commonly conceal themselves " (what a picture for a free
country !), and enacts that the forty days of power of removal shall be counted from the time they give notice to
the overseers of their residence in the parish, which notice
was in 1691 ordered to be read in church, so that the
fugitive might be hunted down by any who objected to
his presence.   The same Act of 1691 did, however, lessen
the burden by establishing derivative settlements, such
as payment of taxes for one year, serving an annual office,
hiring for a year, and apprenticeship.   In connection
with this last, and as a specimen of the spirit of fraudulent selfishness which the law of settlement naturally
aroused in different parishes, it may be mentioned that
in 1758 a law was passed to put down a very base
arrangement, whereby "great numbers of persons have
been unwarily bound apprentices by certain deeds, *not
indented* (*i.e.* not by legal indenture), by which many
of them have suffered great loss and damage on account
of their having been refused a settlement in such parish
where they have been bound, and have been removed to
the parish where their last legal settlement was before
such apprenticeship."   It is indeed a surprising fact that
in England some 130 years ago a man should be driven
by force of law from the place where he had served his
time as an apprentice, and intended to pursue his trade
in peace.

The Third Period.—The administration of Poor Law during the seventy years of this period may be described as the exact antithesis to the first. In *that*, as we have noted, the main object of legislation was to restrict the wages of the labourer for the benefit of the employer; in *this* the object was to maintain the rate of (agricultural) wages at a certain level, no matter whether the employer could afford to give it or not. An opinion got abroad that it was the duty of the State to provide what the State might deem a proper subsistence for the working classes, the origin and fallacy of which have been neatly exposed in the following "syllogism":—

"It is the duty of the Legislature to provide for all the poor (*i.e.* the destitute)."

"All the labouring classes are poor (*i.e.* without property)."

Therefore "It is the duty of the Legislature to provide for all the labouring classes."

The first definite embodiment of this opinion in the law of the land was made in 1795, under circumstances that show how commonly accepted the notion had become. The nation was entering into the agony of the great war with France, prices were rising beyond all past experience, and to keep the people in good humour at any cost had become a State necessity. And so, on May 6, 1795, at Speenhamland, near Newbury (the date and place deserve to be solemnly recorded), the Berkshire magistrates issued an edict in which they declare that they will in future make certain calculations and allowances for the relief of all poor and industrious men and their families, and then proceeded to fix a scale of relief proportioned to the price of wheat and the number of

F

the family.   This is the celebrated "Speenhamland Act
of Parliament," which was immediately followed in many
counties, and much more cheerfully obeyed than is wont
to be the case with the Acts of its more august rival at
Westminster.   Not but what the Berkshire legislators
were merely giving practical shape to the opinions and
proposals, which, though they did not pass into laws,
show what was the state of feeling in the House of
Commons itself.   Mr. Whitbread introduced a Bill
authorising Justices to fix a minimum of wages, as
before (so certain is the law of reaction and retaliation)
they had attempted to fix a maximum ; and subsequently
he complained that upon searching the statute-book he
could find no law to COMPEL THE FARMERS TO DO THEIR
DUTY.   Mr. Fox thought that the magistrates should
protect the poor from the injustice of grasping employers.
Mr. Lechmere opined that no agricultural labourer could
support himself and his family with comfort.   Mr. Pitt,
who evinced a much profounder knowledge of the subject, and who denounced the law of settlement as inter-
fering with the free circulation of labour, and proposed
an annual Poor Law budget to prevent abuses, nevertheless introduced a Bill for authorising allowances out of
the public rates, including the present of a cow or other
domestic animal.

The prevailing ignorance of economical laws is not
altogether excusable, for Adam Smith was but just dead ;
Bentham was alive, and criticised Pitt's proposals with
trenchant severity ; Burke (who, however, died in 1797),
at least knew better, as did probably Pitt himself.   But
it is a melancholy tribute to the power of sentimental
error (palliated by the circumstances of the times) that

all the injury inflicted upon the labouring classes by the deliberately hostile legislation of Plantagenet or Tudor statesmen was but as dust in the balance compared with what they suffered from the benevolent measures of some of the best men that have ever ruled in England. As it has been well expressed : "The poor might well say, We can deal with our enemies, only save us from our friends."

The Poor Law Acts passed during this period are too numerous to be even mentioned, and yet they bear no proportion to the number of propositions made and the amount of discussion evoked. Roughly speaking, the Acts during the eighteenth century part of this seventy-five years were intended to give expression to the new policy of sentimental care for the interests of the poor; while those of the second part were some feeble and illusive attempts to grapple with evils, by the growing extent of which popular opinion was excited, and at length seriously alarmed. We can but allude to some of the more important of them.[1]

We may remark first that the beginning of George III.'s reign was creditably distinguished by a number of measures for the benefit of the working people, which,

[1] Among the many abortive proposals of this period a plan, which received the support of Burke, to enable the "poor" to purchase terminable annuities of the overseers, upon the security of the rates, deserves mention : it shows how the ideas of many modern reforms were started at this time. The scheme of Compulsory Insurance has not even the dubious merit of originality; for in 1786 Mr. Acland proposed that every labourer between twenty and thirty should be compelled to pay 2d. weekly, and women 1½d., as insurance against sickness. The parish authorities were to be treasurers and managers. But it does not appear that this further interference with the liberty of the working classes gained much support.

though partaking more of a charitable or benevolent character than of the nature of Poor Laws, ought to be noticed. Thus pauper children were ordered to be sent not less than five miles out of London to be brought up, and "guardians" appointed to look after them; the duration of apprenticing was diminished from 24 to 21 years of age; parish authorities were punished for making payments in bad money to the poor; regulations were passed for friendly societies, hospitals, lying-in hospitals, penitentiaries, and the apprenticing of children to the king's ships; and finally, by an Act which shows the spirit of the age at its best, an Act of Elizabeth concerning building cottages in rural places (itself at the time a singularly well meaning measure, for it provided that each new cottage should have four acres of land attached to it, and *be inhabited by one family alone*) was repealed upon the ground that it "laid the industrious poor under great difficulties to procure habitations, and in other respects has been found inconvenient to the labouring part of the nation." This sounds plausible enough, but we may suspect that some selfish interests in the way of settlement were at the bottom of it, and certainly the prohibition against overcrowding was repealed.

The principal Poor Law Acts of the close of the eighteenth century concerned the formation of Unions, building and inspection of workhouses, regulations for apprenticing, rating, and the definite establishment of out-relief, to which may be added an alteration in the law of bastardy, tending also to the relaxation of morals.

The first of these was Gilbert's Act in 1782. It recites the great increase of expenditure, and the increased

sufferings of the poor notwithstanding, laying the blame
upon the parochial authorities, from whom it proceeds
to take away the administration of relief in all parishes
which should adopt the new Act.   Power was given to
form Unions or Incorporations by voluntary arrangement
of adjacent parishes, and to build a workhouse for the
Union.   With the customary confidence in the Justices,
it was enacted that they should appoint visitors and
guardians; the latter being paid, and, therefore, resembling the modern relieving officer, and being under the
control of the Justices and visitors (themselves supposed
to be of the social standing of the Justices), by whom the
poor relief administration was carried on.   Sixty-seven
Incorporations were thus formed, some of which, by an
anomaly only possible in England, survive in name to
this day, e.g. at Oxford, and have caused a good deal of
trouble.   The guardians were expressly forbidden to
send any but the "impotent" to the workhouse, and by
an ever-recurring fallacy were ordered to find suitable
employment for the able-bodied near their own homes.
Four years later returns procured by the same Mr.
Gilbert showed that the cost of relief had risen from
£1,529,780 in 1776, to an average of £2,004,238 for
1783-5, being an increase of £474,458, or more than
30 per cent.

In 1790 inspection of poorhouses by the Justices
was ordered, or by other persons, such as clergymen and
doctors, under their authority.   Particular complaint was
made of infectious diseases, and the absence of discipline
and classification was already producing the abuses that
were found to exist forty years later.

Fresh regulations concerning parish apprenticing were

made in 1792, by which penalties were enacted for misusage, such misusage having been in part occasioned by
a deliberate attempt to get rid by discharge of the
apprentices whom the masters had unwillingly received.
Perhaps no part of the old Poor Law was more prolific
of ill-will, craft, and cruelty than this.

The inexcusable rigour of the law of settlement, which
had not escaped the generous indignation of Burke, was
dealt with in 1795 by an Act which finally forbade the
removal of persons from any parish until they had
become actually chargeable to the rates, and which in
all cases enabled the Justices to suspend an order of
removal if the pauper were unfit to travel, because, as the
Act recites, persons were often removed in time of sickness to the danger of their lives.   Glimpses like these
show what hard-hearted cruelty had crept into the
administration of the old Poor Law, and how natural it
is for well meaning but mistaken kindness to produce in
practice the very opposite results to what it intends.

The decisively fatal step of legalising out-relief to the
able-bodied, and in aid of wages, was taken in 1796.   It
will be remembered that an Act of 1722 had established
a kind of workhouse test, and this was now formally
rescinded upon the ground stated in language now
become familiar, "That it was inconvenient and oppressive, inasmuch as it often prevents an industrious poor
person from receiving such occasional relief as is best
suited to his particular case, and in certain cases holds
out conditions of relief injurious to the comfort and
domestic situation and happiness of such poor persons."
Accordingly, the parish authorities were empowered to
give relief to any industrious person at his own residence

in case of sickness or distress—distress being practically
defined as the not having an income which the Justices
thought sufficient. And it was expressly added that
refusal to enter a poorhouse should not be a cause for
withholding relief. Moreover, the Justices were authorised to order relief for a certain time to persons who
"are entitled to ask and receive such relief at their own
houses." The result, of course, was that the "bread-
scales" became a sort of bye-law in every county, and
that what the farmer did not give in wages was made up
from the rates. The labourers, being no longer paid
according to their earnings, rapidly deteriorated, and it
is significant that in one town (Winslow) so early as 1795,
they are described as having become "very lazy and
imperious."

In 1801 recourse was once more had to the infalli-
bility of Justices, who were made the rating, as they
had already become the relieving, authority. They were
authorised not merely as before to quash an illegal rate,
but to amend it by altering names and amounts. And
in order, as the Act passed two years later declares, "to
render Justices of the Peace more safe in the execution
of their duty," the penalty for an illegal decision to be
recovered from a Justice was limited to 2d., unless it was
plain that he was actuated by improper motives. Of
these no one accuses the English magistracy as a body,
nor even of consciously yielding to self-interest in adjudi-
cating upon matters in which they were perhaps the
most interested persons present, but they were placed in
a position of antagonism to the Poor Law officials which
made impartiality impossible, and duties were imposed
upon them which it was out of the question that they

could have the opportunity or the information for dis
charging properly.

The last touch to the picture of industrial demorali-
sation was added in 1809 and 1810, when two Bastardy
Acts were passed with the object—still from the same
sentimental feeling—of favouring the woman at the
expense of the man.   It is difficult to believe, but it is
nevertheless the truth, that by these Acts any woman,
before her child was born, could, upon her mere unsup-
ported oath, cause any man to be sent to prison unless
he could indemnify the parish against any expense in
respect of the child said to be his.   This marks the
lowest point reached by Poor Law legislation, and as
usual, the consequences to the character and position of
the persons, *i.e.* in this case the women, whom it was
desired to protect from the ill effects of their own conduct, were in the long run far more injurious than to
the men, just as the labourer suffered far more from
legislative benevolence than the employer.

After this the nation could but look on in a kind of
paralysis at the inordinate growth of moral abuses, of
industrial disaster, of ruinous expenditure.   The expenditure doubled itself between the years 1783, when it
stood at £2,004,238, and 1803, when it had arisen to
£4,267,965, gradually increasing till it reached in 1817
its maximum, represented by the enormous sum of
£7,870,801 in a population of about 11,000,000.   Curiously enough this was about the sum reached in 1871,
when the population was about doubled, and all the
costly arrangements for asylums, infirmaries, and district
schools were included.

But dissatisfaction grew with the cost; and discussion

by competent persons, of whom Mr. Malthus was the chief, prepared the public mind for a thorough reform upon rational and, what was a new feature in English legislation of that time, scientific principles. An able report of a Committee of the House of Commons in 1817 laid a finger upon the worst blots, and made a variety of useful proposals. The only practical results of any importance were the constitution of select vestries for the administration of relief, who were instructed to distinguish between the "deserving and the idle, extravagant, and profligate poor." Assistant overseers were to be appointed, and the power of Justices to order relief was somewhat curtailed in places where select vestries had been established. Further facilities were created for building workhouses, and for the first time relief might be given on loan. Several places adopted the provisions of this Act, and set an example of what could be done in the way of reform. Amongst these Southwell and Bingham, Cookham and Hatfield, deserve to be mentioned.

We bring this chapter to a close with the mention of an Act of 1828 to provide for the care of pauper lunatics. As there is no class in the world more deserving of compassion and more in need of public relief, it shows how capricious and untrustworthy is a policy directed merely by sentiment, that this was the first occasion in which the State made special provision for this unfortunate class of human beings. As to the rest, this was the state of things down to the reform of 1834. The public funds were regarded as a regular part of the maintenance of the labouring people engaged in agriculture, and were administered by more than 2000 Justices, 15,000 sets of over-

seers, and 15,000 vestries, acting always independently of
each other, and very commonly in opposition, quite uncon-
trolled, and ignorant of the very rudiments of political
economy.   And the £7,000,000 or more of public money
was the price paid for converting the free labourer into a
slave, without reaping even such returns as slavery can
give.   The able-bodied pauper was obliged to live where
the law of settlement placed him, to receive the income
which the neighbouring magistrates thought sufficient,
to work for the master and in the way which the parish
authorities prescribed, and very often to marry the wife
they found for him.   He was, in short, as has been truly
said of him, a "work of art, and not the natural offspring
of the English race."

CHAPTER IV.

POOR LAW REFORM.

In February 1834 was published perhaps the most remarkable and startling document to be found in the whole range of English, perhaps, indeed, of all, social history. It was the Report upon the administration and practical operation of the Poor Laws by the Commissioners who had been appointed to investigate the subject. In the list of nine gentlemen who composed the Commission there is not to be found a single ornamental name, the Bishop of London (Blomfield), who heads the list, having a deserved reputation for practical sagacity and powers of business. Mr. Sturges Bourne represented the older Poor Law reformers, while the names of Mr. Nassau Senior and Mr. Edwin Chadwick (the future Secretary to the Board) are better known to more recent times. It was their rare good fortune not only to lay bare the existence of abuses and trace them to their roots, but also to propound and enforce the remedies by which they might be cured. It is seldom indeed, that the conditions of so vast and sweeping a reform are found co-existing. The evils were gross and alarming; there was a ministry that had been carried into power by an outburst of reforming zeal; above all, there was a readiness to be guided by principles of purely scientific legislation,

which at a later period gave us Free Trade, Financial
Reform, Colonial Administration, Tithe Commutation,
and the beginning of Law Reform, and for which the
exigencies of parliamentary government, and the over-
flowings of passion and sentiment, allow but too small
and limited a scope. Their success was therefore at once
inevitable and deserved.

The Report opens with these words :—" It is now our
painful duty to report that the fund which the 43d of
Elizabeth directed to be employed in setting to work
children and persons capable of labour, but using no daily
trade, and in the necessary relief of the impotent, is
applied to purposes opposed to the letter, and still more
to the spirit, of that law, and destructive to the morals
of that most numerous class, and to the welfare of all."
It is a duty, which, even at this distance of time, is also
painful, to give the briefest possible sketch of the results
of their investigation. And this not merely because it
is the only way of understanding the need and nature of
the remedies they proposed, but because the Report
ought to be known (by students of social science in the
original) by the general public as a picture of the condition to which a mistaken course of legislation, together
with obstructive and selfish ignorance, can reduce the
greatest nations at the very height of their power and
fame.

I. The Officials by whom the Poor Law was
then administered.—These were the overseers, vestries,
and magistrates. The former were taken from the shop-
keeping or farming class, and served not even for a year
but for six, three, or even two months, so that they had

no opportunity, even if desirous, of introducing regularity
into the administration. The office was disagreeable,
unpopular, and unpaid, and specially obnoxious to busy
men. There were no books kept by which the cost of the
relief, or the reasons of giving it, could be examined,
the only check being that of submitting the mere items
of moneys paid to the vestry, and getting them allowed
by the Justices. Against partiality, favouritism, and
jobbing there was no check; against embezzlement very
little. If the overseers refused relief, the pauper could
summon them before the magistrate, whose order they
must obey; but a more dreaded tribunal at the beer-shop,
with a more stringent procedure in the way of arson and
violence, was at hand to compel obedience. They were
"as a body found wholly incompetent," "anxious to get
through the year with as little unpopularity and trouble
as possible." Their duties were delegated to wives,
children, and shopmen. Tradesmen were obliged to
yield to demands for doles upon pain of losing custom,
nor were assaults at all uncommon. Lastly, in very
many cases the men charged with these responsible
duties were barely able to read and write.[1]

[1] May we lighten up a gloomy subject by some extracts from
Sir F. Head's witty, and, at the same time, instructive article in
the *Quarterly Review*, No. 106. Here is an overseer's answer to a
circular of the Poor Law Commission requiring information :—"It
will never do we any good to alter the law in our parish, as our
parishs very small and there is no probabilitis of alter our kearse
at all. There is no persons fitter to manage the parish better than
ourselves.—T. T., *oversear*."
In answer to an inquiry why a shilling was paid for tolling the
bell at every pauper's death, the overseer replied in a whisper,
"Why, sir, the clerk is a dreadful man, and always threatens to
fight me whenever I wants to stop that ere charge."

The vestries, whether open or representative, were of
the same class as the overseers, though with less sense of
responsibility and more pride of office. They rendered
no account, were not obliged to keep any record of the
members present, or of their speeches and votes, and had
a direct interest in giving relief in aid of earnings. In
particular, a dead set was made at the tithe owners, and
there were several cases in which wages were lowered,
and rates increased for the express purpose of throwing

It is somewhat unfair to quote the following story, for the
heroine of it, if she be alive,—as, for her praiseworthy exertions to
do her duty, she fully deserves to be,—would still be far below three
score years and ten ; but as a picture of the times it is irresistible.
The Assistant Commissioner "found himself in a carpeted parlour,
seated at a large oak table, with the parish accountant by his side.
She was the yeoman's sister, a fine, ruddy, healthy, blooming,
bouncing girl of eighteen. As her plump, red finger went down
the items, it was constantly deserting its official duties to lay aside
a profusion of long black ringlets, which occasionally gamboled
before her visitor's eyes. She had evidently taken great pains to
separate, as cleverly as she could, the motley claimants on the
parish purse, just as her brother had divided his lambs from his
pigs, and his sheep from his cows. She had one long list of
'labourers with families ;' 'widows' were demurely placed in one
corner of her ledger ; 'cesses' stood in another ; vagrants or
trampers crossed one page ; those receiving constant relief sat still
in another ; at last the accountant came to two very long lists—
one was composed of what she called *low* women ; the other, veiled
by her curls, she modestly muttered were '*hilly*jittimites.'"

The governor of a large workhouse was asked to show his
"dietary." He slowly led the way to the dining-hall, and, point-
ing to the paupers' dining-table, said, "Here it is, sir."

Another did not know how many inmates there were in the
house, for whom he was, at the moment, serving up dinner, but
was quite sure that an old blind pauper—one Mrs. Smith—who
"had such a capital memory," could answer the question, which
she at once did.

part of the payment of wages upon their heads.[1]   A
common remark was, " Why should the farmers keep the
labourers to save the gentry and householders?"   A
competent witness declared that the farmers would rather
pay 75 per cent in poor rates, and 25 per cent in wages,
than in the inverse proportions.   Scandalous scenes at
vestry meetings were common, and in the larger places
the higher classes ceased to attend.

The real pivot, however, upon which the system turned
was the Justices.   Their position was that of charitable
gentlemen to whom the oppressed poor could appeal
against the tyranny of the overseers.   In the first place,
they fixed the "scale" of income that every labourer
ought to have, adjusting it with great nicety to the
price of bread and the size of his family.   In the Speenhamland "scale," if the gallon of bread was 1s., a single
man's income was 3s., husband and wife 4s. 6d., and
1s. 6d. for every child up to seven, making 15s. for the
whole family.   And against this order there was of
course no appeal.   In cases of dispute a pauper could
select his own tribunal—that is, the magistrate with
the best character for charity, which often meant timidity
or desire of popularity—and appear before him as an
injured man dragging his oppressor to justice.   It is
needless to say that the magistrate could not have the
same means of ascertaining a man's earnings as the parish
officers, and was easily imposed upon by false representa-
tions.   The paupers would drag the overseer to a favourite
magistrate, passing by the house of another not supposed
to be lenient, "would beat him as usual," and return in

---

[1] This was called fighting the parson, and must have been an
effective mode of warfare.

triumph with music and favours. Of one magistrate it was said that it would pay the parish to give him £100 a year not to act.

Several pages of the Report are taken up with an account of an extraordinary state of things at the Worship Street Police Court, where the overseers and the magistrate had fallen out. The latter insisted upon relief being given in every case, and declared that it was quite impossible to investigate the cases of forty or fifty paupers every day. The overseer retaliated by allowing himself to be summoned for fifty persons at once, and insisting upon each case being heard on its merits. After hearing the first few, the overseer, "seeing the magistrate getting angry," offered to take them into the house for the night, and departed, escorted by two beadles, and followed by his train of paupers, all of whom except ten or twelve slunk away before they reached the house, though they had sworn to the magistrate they were starving. By far the greater part were known bad characters. And this in London!

It is right to add that the Report (dealing in this respect much more gently with magistrates than overseers, for whom also excuses might be pleaded), expressly declares that there is no question as to their good intentions, and that their mistakes are due to misapprehension of the proper objects of the Poor Law, and to their unfitness, by reason of their social position and opportunities of investigating the cases, for the jurisdiction imposed upon them.

II. OUTDOOR RELIEF.—Six methods of giving out relief were discovered by the commission.

(*a*) Relief in kind, consisting chiefly of payment of rent and of tickets for clothing and goods, most often at the shops of vestrymen and overseers.

(*b*) Relief without Labour.—This was a payment either of two or three shillings a week without conditions, or else a rather larger sum given upon condition that the labourers should be confined in a certain place, *e.g.* the Pound or gravel pit, or should attend a roll-call several times a day.   The object appears partly to have labourers within call, if wanted; partly to make things disagreeable to them.   The books of Hampton Poyle, a tiny village near Oxford, contain the following :—" Paid for men and boys standing in the Pound six days, £6 : 7s.

" W. Wheeler" standing in the Pound six days, 8s.

(*c*) Allowance.—This is the amount paid to make up the pauper's income to the " scale " approved by the justices.   Sometimes the earnings were inquired into, more often payment was allowed for each child, under the title of " head money."   Very frequently the rate of wages was fixed at vestry meetings, with allowances to make it up.   Labourers used to get married and go from the church to the overseer, and request to have a house found for them.   A man might earn 21s. a fortnight and then apply to have the average made up for the month. Another man with six children could earn upon an average 9s. per week, but had only earned 5s. from his master and 2s. for work from the parish.   He received as a matter of course 7s. 6d. across the pay table. " Bread money " was regarded as a right, and the wages supposed to be earned were calculated at the lowest rate paid in the district, so that a man might earn by special work £1 a week, and yet receive the extra as per scale.

G

Sometimes large earnings were made in the summer, and the whole parish came on to the rates in the winter. So thoroughly understood was it that the birth of a child entitled to the parish allowance, that the happy father would give notice to the overseer that the birth of a new little pauper might be expected in due time. If the case came before the magistrate, the regular enquiry was, "At what number does the allowance begin in your parish?"

(d) The Roundsman. — This system, which, from an antiquarian point of view, might be interesting as being a mixed survival of primitive communism and mediæval serfdom, consisted in the parish paying the farmers to employ the labourers. The parish sold the commodity of labour to the farmer, and made up the difference between his wages and the income supposed to be his due out of the rates. In one place there was a weekly sale, at which an eyewitness saw ten men knocked down to one farmer for 5s. It was called the ticket system, because the pauper received a ticket from the overseer as a warrant for the farmer to employ him at the cost of the parish. The "roundsman" often spent the day in going from house to house for employment, the farmers certifying that he had called at their houses, in order to justify the overseer in paying him.

(e) Parish Employment. — This (which was the only legal form of out-relief[1]) was not frequently adopted, though it was the only reasonable form that out-relief could take. It meant the employment of labourers on the roads or in the workhouse, and it was obviously easier to give relief gratuitously than to exact labour for

---

[1] There was a decision of Lord Tenterden that an overseer must provide work, if possible, before giving relief.

it. Moreover, the necessity of associating the paupers
in large gangs worked very disastrous results. Most of
the day was spent in idleness, and an attempt to put a
superintendent over the work was promptly met by a
successful threat to drown him. The paupers claimed
a right (before the Justices) to work less hours for the
parish than for private employers, and in many places
received higher pay than they could earn as wages. If
a man showed signs of doing his task work, the obvious
remark by his companions was, "You must have your
money whether you work or not."

(f) The Labour Rate.—This was an agreement that
each ratepayer should employ at a fixed rate so many
"settled" labourers, or else pay the amount of their
wages to the overseer. In one case the names of the
occupiers were put in a bag and drawn out by each
labourer, who had then to work for that master for the
week at 10s., and for another the next; the farmer, of
course, being under strong inducement to discharge his
regular workmen, in order to find work for the labourers
thus quartered upon him. In one parish the rector was
required to employ $62\frac{1}{2}$ men at 10s. per week, besides
his poor rate of £420, an amount which was about
double the value of his benefice.

We shall, however, endeavour presently to group together the various abuses to which the system of out-
relief gave rise; but before doing so, we must mention
one matter by which the evils of Poor Law were then,
as they always have been, greatly aggravated.

III. SETTLEMENT.—Although the Poor Law administrators paid little attention to law or principles, there

was one fixed rule that was never transgressed. They
never gave permanent relief to labourers who had no
settlement in the parish, nor to their own settled people
if they were residing elsewhere. The reason of course
was, that each parish, though willing to pay rates in aid
of wages for its own supposed benefit, was not very
likely to be willing to pay the wages of persons employed elsewhere. Every labourer was therefore bound
to his own parish, not as in the preceding century by
the law, *i.e.* the operation of the Act of Charles II., for
that, as we have seen, had been repealed; but by the
fixed practice of Poor Law administration, which gave
him large "allowances" and other payments, only upon
condition that his settlement gave him a claim upon the
parish for relief. There was thus great need that the
law of settlement should be as simple and intelligible
as possible; instead of which the ingenuity of the law
itself never accomplished a more perfect network of
intricacies and difficulties. The explanation, so characteristic of English legislation, is this: We have seen
that the Act of Charles II. allowed overseers to remove
any new-comer within 40 days of his first appearance in
the parish. We have seen, also, that to mitigate the
rigour of this enactment, an Act of William and Mary
allowed derivative settlements, such as apprenticeships,
hiring for a year, renting a tenement, and so on. Then
came the Act of George III., which did away with the
rigour of the Act of Charles by making persons irremovable until they became actually chargeable. Logically,
the secondary modes of settlement should also have been
abolished at that time also, but they were retained,
causing infinite trouble and legal difficulties. For as

each new settlement, when acquired, destroyed the old one, every effort was made by parish officers to prevent one from being obtained, or to establish one elsewhere. Here is an illustration which seems hardly credible. A man leaves parish A at the age of 15, goes to London, lives there many years, has a family, becomes destitute there, having acquired no settlement, owing to his work being upon jobs. He is passed back to parish A, which discovers that he was hired as a groom for one year before going to London, and lived with his master six weeks at a seaside place in Wales, when, if it could be shown that he slept at least 40 nights in the hotel, he would become chargeable to that parish B,—neither A nor B having had anything whatever to do with him for 30 or 40 years.

We shall now endeavour to sum up the actual effects of Poor Law administration upon the welfare of the people, and, merely owing to the necessity of imposing some limit, shall confine ourselves to a dozen heads.

(1.) *The burden upon rateable property.*—The typical, though, it must also be admitted, the extreme case quoted by the Report is that of Cholesbury, in Buckinghamshire, where the rates, which had been £10 : 11s. in 1801, were proceeding in 1832 at the amount of £367, when they ceased, owing to the impossibility of collecting more. The poor rate had swallowed up the whole value of the land, which was going out of cultivation. The paupers meanwhile were supported by rates in aid and voluntary benevolence; and it is obvious that however small might be the actual confiscation of property in that village, it must, by the nature of the case, spread, since every acre that ceased to support the inhabitants

threw fresh burdens upon those that were left to do so.
But when we remember that the amount raised in poor
rates was over £6,000,000, we can imagine that the
margin between possession and confiscation was growing
perilously small. Farms were in all districts without
tenants, simply because it was found impossible to pay
rates that were perhaps £1 per acre. And the general
opinion as to the approach of absolute ruin was thus
graphically expressed : "The eighteen-penny children
will eat up this parish in ten years more, unless some
relief be afforded us."

(2.) *The burden upon the poorer ratepayers.*—Their case
was hard indeed. In many instances they earned less
and worked harder than the paupers whom they were
supporting in idleness and comparative luxury. It
sometimes happened that the overseer called for rates
upon men who had at that moment nothing to eat in
the house. As one witness said, "Poor is the diet of
the pauper; poorer is the diet of the small ratepayer;
poorest is the diet of the independent labourer."

(3.) *The burden upon independent labourers.*—Perhaps
no more really shocking result of the system was than
that industrious men who were trying to maintain themselves could not obtain employment. In attempting to
abolish the law of nature, which punishes improvidence
and idleness, the Poor Law succeeded in abolishing that
other law which rewards virtue and thrift. Repeated
cases occur in which men of excellent character were
superseded by paupers who, as they must be maintained
somehow, it was thought good should be set to work.
If an industrious man was known to have laid by money
he would be left without work till his savings were spent.

Sometimes such men were discharged till they were reduced to the desired state. Men who deferred marriage had not the same chance of obtaining employment as youths with families. Not many years before this date to be a "parish bird" was accounted disgraceful; not to be so was now thought foolish. Here is a specimen of indignant rustic eloquence,—"The paupers blame me for what I do. They say to me, 'What are you working for?' I say, 'For myself.' They say, 'You are only doing it to save the parish, and if you didn't do it you would get the same as another man has, and would get the money for smoking your pipe and doing nothing.' 'Tis a hard thing for a man like me."

(4.) *The burden upon non-employers.*—We have already noticed that the poor rate being levied upon house property and tithes was *pro tanto* a rate paid by other than employers in aid of wages. The same thing obtained in manufactories, where employers sometimes received annual payments from the parish for keeping their paupers at work. To take an instance. At Nottingham the masters reduced the rate of wages for stocking making, giving their men a certificate to the effect that they were only earning (say) 6s. a week. The men then applied to the parish, who allowed them 4s. or 5s. more.[1]

(5.) *The demoralization of the officials.*—"The rental" (it has been said—*Edinburgh Review*, No. 149) "of a pauperized parish was like the revenue of the Sultan of

---

[1] The Labour Rate was very popular with the farmers, because it threw the burden upon shopkeepers and other non-employers. The hardship upon small farmers, doing their own work, was intolerable.

Turkey—a prey of which every administrator hoped to
get a share. The owner of cottage property found in
the parish a liberal and solvent tenant, and the petty
shopkeeper and publican attended the vestry to vote
allowances to his customers and debtors." The pay
ment of rent was so universal (to prevent homes being
broken up and families thrown into the workhouse) that a
brisk speculation sprang up in cottage property of a low
type. This was aggravated by the custom of not rating
the smaller tenements, a practice that became fruitful of
abuse and jobbery. But the reader must imagine all
this, or find it in the Report for himself.

(6.) *Chicanery and litigation.*—This was a direct consequence of the law of settlement. Cottages were pulled
down, and the inhabitants bribed to sleep in adjoining
parishes. Fraudulent hirings were made for 364 days, so
as to break settlement by annual hiring. Apprentices
were bound out in other parishes so as to shift the settlement. Men were bribed to marry women of the worst
character for the same purpose, and the overseers were
accustomed to negotiate marriages where a child was
expected, the father of which (as the woman would say)
does not belong to you. Landlords pulled down sometimes every cottage on their estate so as to compel sur-
rounding parishes to pay for the work done on their
property. In one case a proprietor of a parish hired a
farm in the parish of Ely, and sent his own people to
work on it in yearly batches, and then turned them off
with a settlement gained in that parish. And many
cases of similar abuses are reported. Fraud and perjury
abounded.

(7.) *Disorganization of industry.*—This was also due to

settlement. Any chance event—say the establishment or closing of a manufacture—changed the proportion between the settled labourers and the number required for work in that locality. And Irish labourers had opportunities of obtaining work over Englishmen, because the latter did not dare to leave their places of settlement, which "appeared to them like leaving their freeholds or heir-looms." Instances are recorded where steady men without families declined tempting situations that would have doubled their income, for fear of losing their settlement.

(8.) *Deterioration of labour.*—The loss of farmers, by whom so much must be trusted to the care of their workmen (as contrasted with manufactories, where there is more superintendence), was set down as enormous. This points to the truth that the agricultural labourer ought to be, and perhaps, in spite of appearance, *is*, the most *skilled* labourer there is. The conditions of his work are such as that, if they drag the *man* down, the work itself elevates the workman. Very much must be left to his care, his experience, and his trustworthi-ness. But not only had he become unskilful and dis-honest, but positively hostile to his employer, and desirous of doing him injury. Nor, considering that the parish was his real mainstay, is this to be wondered at.

(9.) *Deterioration of morals.*—This, of which the Report gives long and melancholy instances, must be taken for granted. No words of ours could do justice to it. To borrow the aid of alliteration, drink and dissipation, indolence and insolence, deception and dependence, had become the familiar characteristics of the men from whose ranks had come the soldiery who had astonished all Europe. In fact all the healthy laws, customs, and motives that bind society together were in this instance broken and cast aside. "There was never a better illustration of the truth that in morals as well as in political economy the laws of nature are wiser than those of man, and that the virtues of the mass of the people are as much at the mercy of the Legislature as their wealth — equally capable of injury from rash interference, and of recovery when that interference has ceased."

(10.) *The destruction of family ties.*—That part of the Act of Elizabeth which directed the maintenance of the impotent by relatives was very seldom enforced, with the consequence that "persons had no scruple in asking to be paid for the performance of those domestic duties which the most brutal savages are in general willing to render to their own kindred." Payments for looking after sick or aged parents were not at all uncommon. And it may be added that inasmuch as the law still allows impotent folk to be kept out of the house by the parish, traces of this feeling are still to be found. So certain is the operation of law in morals as in nature !

(11.) *Improvident marriages.*—Allusion has been already made to this evil, of which instances have been known, where the married couple left the church for the work-house. But it reappears also as part of the consequences of the law of bastardy, which is the last and most shocking abuse upon our melancholy list.

(12.) The earlier legislation in the time (eighteenth year) of Elizabeth upon the subject of bastardy had wisely contented itself with prescribing that in order to prevent illegitimate children from becoming chargeable

to the parish (which is all that Poor Laws have to deal
with), and so "defrauding of the relief of the aged and
impotent true poor of the same parish," the justices
should compel the parents to support their child.   An
Act of James I., however, ordered the mother of an
illegitimate child to be punished with imprisonment and
hard labour.   This failing,—as all attempts to treat vice
as punishable crime must in the long run fail,—the Act
of George III., previously mentioned, tried to punish the
father by compelling the Justices to commit to prison,
until he should have indemnified the parish from all
charges, any man against whom a woman should swear an
ex parte information that he was the father of her (as
yet) unborn child.   The actual operation of the law at
the time we are speaking had come, under the stress of
popular sentimentalism, to be as follows :—The Justices
made an order that both parents should pay to the parish
a weekly sum to maintain the child.   The sum assessed
on the woman was scarcely ever, if ever, exacted ; the
sum received from the man was paid over by the overseers to the woman, and if he were in default the parish
made up the amount.   To the woman, therefore, the child
was little or no burden ; to the man, upon whom she
elected to swear it, being very often bribed by the real
father, or even encouraged by the parish officers to
choose a man able to pay, it often meant ruin so complete that he had to elect between fleeing the locality
or marrying a woman who had in many cases either
sworn falsely against him, or else for her own purposes
tempted him to vice.

The consequences of this interference with nature's
law, that the shame and burden of illegitimacy shall de-

volve mainly upon the woman, are too shocking to be detailed in these pages: suffice it to say, that it was another example of the ruin which human folly, trying to be wise above what is written in nature's book, can bring upon the class or sex it seeks to benefit. Profligacy became a lucrative occupation, inasmuch as what the mother of two or three illegitimate children received from the fathers enabled her to live more comfortably than most decent families, more especially in the very common cases where the children were utterly neglected; nay, she was "considered a good object of marriage on account of these weekly payments," the proceeds of the sale of virtue becoming in this way a marriage portion! But enough of this: let the evidence of one witness out of many serve to illustrate the whole. "The daughters of some farmers, and even landowners, have bastard children, who keep their daughters and children with them, and regularly keep back their poor rate to meet the parish allowance for their daughters' bastards. We have no doubt the same grievance exists in many other parishes."

IV. INDOOR RELIEF.—The condition of the workhouses is not very fully gone into in the Report itself, though the appendix containing the evidence of the witnesses examined enables us to see clearly how entirely the opinion of the Commissioners was justified, "that indoor relief, as given within the walls of the poorhouse, is also subject to great mal-administration." A published account of one workhouse, by Mr. Chadwick, had excited great attention, and the Commissioners state that in their opinion, in respect of the absence of classification, dis-

cipline, and employment, and of the extravagance of the
allowances, it was only a specimen of ordinary work
houses in similar towns. We shall, however, at this
point leave the Report, and quote from the account of
an eyewitness as contained in the *Quarterly Review* article
(No. 106), to which previous reference has been made.
The humour and dramatic power with which it is written,
albeit such qualities appear mournfully out of place in
such a scene, make it well worthy of perusal.

"To give our readers a full and correct notion of the
poorhouses in East Kent would be almost as difficult as
to sketch him a picture of the variegated surface of the
globe. . . Some are lofty, some low, but all (*i.e.* those built
under Gilbert's Act) are massive and costly. . . One
might be called an elegant retreat, splendidly contrasted
with the mean little ratepaying hovels at its feet, which,
like a group of wheelbarrows round the Lord Mayor's
coach are lost in the splendour of the gilded spectacle. . .
Others again are composed of old farmhouses, more or
less out of repair. Some are supported by props; many
are really unsafe . . . and are so dilapidated, so bent
by the prevailing wind, that it seems a problem whether
the worn-out, aged inmate will survive his wretched
hovel, or it him."

"In some of the largest of these habitations an
attempt has been made to classify and arrange the inmates, and, generally speaking, every apartment is exceedingly clean. In one large room are found sitting in
silence a group of motionless, worn-out men, with age
grown double, with nothing to do, with nothing to cheer
them, with nothing in this world to hope for, gnarled
into all sorts of attitudes, so that they look more like

pieces of ship timber than men. In another room are
seen huddled together a number of old exhausted women,
clean, tidy, but speechless and deserted. Whenever we
asked whether they were often visited we invariably received the same reply, 'Oh no! people seldom takes any
notice of 'em after they once gets here.'

"Going through the sick wards, as we passed one poor
man he said he knew he was dying, and, raising his
head from his pillow, begged hard that 'little George'
might be sent for; but the master, accustomed to such
scenes, would have considered the request inadmissible,
had not the Assistant Commissioner ventured rather
strongly to enforce it.

"On descending the staircase the next scene was a
room full of sturdy labourers out of work; these were
generally sitting round a stove, with their faces scorched
and half roasted; as we passed them they never rose
from their seats, and had generally an overfed, a
mutinous, and an insubordinate appearance. A room
full of girls of from five to sixteen, and another of boys
of the same ages, completed the arrangements," and it is
added that separation was only nominally enforced. So
much for the *larger* houses.

"In the smaller ones classification has been found
impossible; all that is effected is to put the males of all
ages into one room, and all the females into another.
In these cases the old are teased by the children, who
are growled at when they talk, and scolded when they
play, until they become cowed into silence. The able-
bodied men are the noisy orators of the room; the
children listen to their oaths, and, what is often much
worse, to the substance of their conversation; while

a poor idiot or two, hideously twisted, stands grin-
ning at the scene, or, in spite of remonstrances, inces-
santly chattering to himself.   In the women's hall,
which is generally separated only by a passage from the
men's, females of all characters and of all shapes live
with infants, children, and young girls of all ages." . . .
"A large attic used as a dormitory for married couples,"
completes the description.

"In the small tottering hovels we found generally
seven or eight old people at the point of death, an able-
bodied labourer or two, with a boy or a young girl, who
was generally said to be 'only a love child.'   Sometimes
we discovered but two or three inmates in these diminu-
tive poor huts ; there was, however, always a being
termed the governor ; and in one case we found only two
paupers, one being his Excellency, and the other his guest.

" ' And so his man Friday kept his house neat and tidy,
For you know 'twas his duty to do so ;
Like brother and brother, who live one with another,
So lived Friday and Robinson Crusoe.'"

If the question be naturally asked, why people con-
sented to inhabit these places, the answer is, that they
were bribed into them by the promise of abundance of
food.   "Everywhere the Kentish pauper has three, four,
or five 'meat days' per week; his bread is many degrees
better than that given to our soldiers ; he has vegetables
at discretion ; and in the larger houses the boast is, 'We
gives 'em as much victuals as ever they can eat.'"

"In Kent, stall-fed charity, in order to bait the workhouse trap, arranged, printed, and published a bribe,
which we consider as one of the most astonishing documents in the pig-sty history of our Poor Laws."

This document is the contract for providing workhouse fare, from which we gather that the contractors were to furnish, *inter alia*, "warm, wholesome, sweet, clean, comfortable beds; servants to cook and serve the victuals, and attend on the poor; good, sweet, wholesome fat meat, good sound small beer, best flour, good Gloucester cheese, good and clean butter." Pork and salt meat were forbidden. Bacon and fish were allowed as a variety. The fires were to be good, and kept up in certain rooms at all hours, so that the paupers might boil their tea-kettles. Lastly, the contractors were "to PROVIDE WIGS for such as wear them or require them."

This, we think, is enough, and more than justifies the moral with which the Assistant Commissioner concluded his address, to the labouring classes of the county of Kent: "the hanger on ought not to be raised higher than him on whom he hangs."

The above description will serve to show the nature of the abuses with which the Poor Law Commissioners had to deal, and will therefore explain the remedies which they suggested. As these were practically embodied in the Poor Law Amendment Act, which is the system now in force, we need only mention the principal reforms which they recommended. Some of these, it may be added, had already been tried with success.

(1.) All relief to able-bodied persons, except in well-regulated workhouses, to be declared illegal. This is the celebrated "workhouse test."

(2.) The appointment of a Central Board to control the administration, to frame and enforce regulations as to giving relief, and to make those regulations uniform.

(3.) The formation of Unions of parishes, according

to the discretion of the Central Board, to provide and
build a common workhouse for the district; each parish,
however, to pay for its own poor, and to pay for the
establishment charges (*i.e.* the house and officers), according to the average cost of its own paupers. I (This looks
as though the Commissioners expected the entire cessa-
tion, in time, of out-relief.)

(4.) Certain regulations as to uniformity of accounts,
appointment and removal of officers, furnishing of sup-
plies by contract,—all intended to put down serious
abuses.

(5.) Alterations in the law of apprenticing, to be
made by the Central Board, as their future experience
may determine.

(6.) The same as to vagrants, with the view of
making their relief to be such as only the destitute will
accept. They are hopeless as to the benefit of express
enactments.

(7.) All settlements to be abolished, except by parent-
age, till children are sixteen; by marriage in the case of
women; and by birth, *i.e.* the place where any person
shall have been first known to have existed, in all other
cases. (This recommendation was not altogether carried
out in the Act, which retained settlement by residence
for one year, provided the person paid the poor rates,
and, in deference to common law, settlement by property if the owner lived within ten miles.)

(8.) All punishment of parents of illegitimate children
to be abolished, as being worse than useless, and the
whole matter to be taken out of the province of Poor
Law by the enactment that the child shall follow until
sixteen the settlement of the only known parent, *i.e.* the

mother, who is also to be made irremovable, unless she
asks for relief.   If she does apply, the relief for the
child is to be considered as relief to the mother, as in
the case of widows. ʃ (The Act, however, while throwing
upon the mother the burden of providing for her child till
the age of sixteen, or upon her husband, if she marries,
prescribed that if the child became chargeable, the overseers might apply to the Justices, who, if they were
satisfied by sufficient corroborative evidence, might
make an order upon the father to pay a certain weekly
sum,[1] no part of which should be applicable to the support of the mother.   With this, which only extends the
general Poor Law principle of responsibility of relations
to the case of illegitimacy, bastardy ceases to be a
special part of Poor Law administration, and further
mention of the subject may be spared.)

The Bill founded upon these recommendations was
read a second time in the House of Commons on the 9th
of May 1834, by a majority of 299 votes to 20.   It was,
however, modified during its progress by clauses meant
to restrict the power of the Central Board, and its duration limited to five years.   It was introduced into the
House of Lords by Lord Brougham, and supported by
the Duke of Wellington, and carried on the second
reading against a minority of 13 votes.

In 1838 the Act was extended to Ireland, where, as
there had been no Poor Law at all, the whole system
had to be created from the beginning.   The Irish
Poor Law was substantially the same as the English,

---

[1] No part of the new Poor Law was more fiercely attacked than
this, and strong efforts were made either to modify it, or so to
administer this clause as to punish the man, or provide a civil
remedy for the woman.

with this important modification, that out-relief was altogether prohibited, a fact which would seem to show, if proof were needed, that out-relief is not a necessary part of Poor Law administration. A somewhat melancholy commentary upon the system of out-relief is afforded by the fact that in 1859 there were five paupers in Scotland [1] (of all countries in the world!) for one in Ireland, and twelve in the Highlands to one in Ulster and Connaught. (Sir John M'Neill in the Fourteenth Annual Report, Scotland.)

The new Poor Law was introduced in Scotland in 1845, but no attempt can be made to deal with the subject of Scotch Poor Law in this volume.[1] It would, however, be impossible to pass over the name of Dr. Chalmers in any treatise concerning the Poor Law, which he opposed so strenuously, and for a while so successfully. The circumstances are briefly these :—

The old Scottish Poor Law was based upon a statute of 1579, and bore a close resemblance to the earlier legislation of Queen Elizabeth, by which the church-officers in each parish were to provide for the destitute by means of semi-voluntary assessments. In England, as we have seen, owing to divisions in the Church and to the supremacy of the State, the further step was taken of creating legal means of relief separate from ecclesiastical authorities ; but in Scotland, where these conditions did not prevail, the law remained as it was. The Kirk-Sessions, that is, the ministers and elders, had the ordinary management of the parochial poor, and the con-

[1] The best authority on Scotch Poor Law is said to be *The Scottish Poor Laws*, by Scotus, Edinburgh, 1870, a book I have not seen.

trol over the weekly collections and other subscriptions.
This was the state of things which Dr. Chalmers, having
a strong aversion to Poor Law, and especially to the
form which it had assumed in England before 1834,
revived in his parish at Glasgow; the Church taking
charge of the poor, upon a system of minute investigation and moral aid, much resembling the Elberfeld experiment, of which it may claim to be the forerunner.
The system was as successful in the one town as in the
other, but depended upon the influence of one man; and
it is said that in the rest of Scotland the relief of the
poor was very inadequate and partial. Accordingly, the
Act of 1845 formed a central Board of Supervision,
composed of the chief magistrates of certain large towns,
together with members nominated by the Crown; and
under their management most of the parishes have
accepted the principle of compulsory assessment, and
have elected Parochial Boards to take charge of poor
relief. Poorhouses have been established upon the
English model; and the diet, at any rate in respect of
luxuries, made inferior to that of the self-sustaining
labourer.

It is but right to add that that part of Dr. Chalmers'
arguments against Poor Laws which was founded upon
the attractiveness of great and elaborate systems upon the
poor, so as to draw them to ask for out-relief, has been
abundantly justified by experience. The pauperizing
effects of the new Poor Law were found to be considerable, contrary to what happened in England, outdoor
relief being the rule in proportion of twelve to one.
(See a paper read before the British Association in 1871
by Mr. Peterkin, Superintendent of the Poor.)

CHAPTER V.

POOR LAW ADMINISTRATION.

WE are now to give the reader some idea of the actual
working of the Poor Law at this present moment,
noting as we proceed the principal alterations that have
been made since the new Poor Law came into existence. The main outlines of the system are perhaps not
very difficult of comprehension, but the details, especially
the legal questions, are very elaborate and perplexing,
and there are perhaps few subjects upon which legal
opinion has been more often taken. The mass of literature in the shape of reports, discussions, speeches, and
law books, is enormous; and it is perhaps not the least
serious charge that can be brought against the Poor Law
that it has absorbed, it may be in artificial channels, so
large a share of human industry, ingenuity, and ability.
And if the outward appearance of the system be simple
and its working smooth, it is only by reason of careful
attention to an immense variety of unnoticed details,
and also of deference to certain principles or arrangements which have established themselves after prolonged
inquiry and discussion by some of the ablest men in
England. And yet, as it will be our duty in the following pages to point out, nothing like finality can be said

to have been arrived at, while the cost of pauperism and number of paupers remain what they are.

We shall break up this chapter into five parts, namely the Central Authority, the Local Authorities, Out-Relief, Indoor Relief, and the present state of the Law of Settlement, with which is connected the areas over which contributions are raised by local rating. It must, however, be borne in mind that the subjects of central and local government, together with the method of providing for the national expenditure, belong to other books in this series, and are only treated here so far as some acquaintance with them is necessary to the clearer understanding of Poor Law administration.

PART I.—THE CENTRAL AUTHORITY.

The existing Poor Law Central Authority, now called the Local Government Board, has grown by three successive changes out of the original Poor Law Commission formed in 1834. The first change, which might be almost called a crisis, took place at the end of the five years for which the Commission was originally established. The strong and general reaction which ensued upon the heroic reform legislation of the previous years culminated in so fierce an attack upon the Poor Law Amendment that it remained doubtful for some years whether this part of the reforming measures would not have to be, in part at least, sacrificed as a kind of expiatory victim for the rest. The Commissioners had in a few years almost transformed the face of the country, and no rational person could doubt the good they had accomplished. But they had been brought into conflict with the selfishness, timidity,[1] and obstructiveness of local authorities, not only of those whom they had superseded, but of those whom they had created, and who in certain places, *e.g.* Bolton, Nottingham, and Macclesfield,[2] had been elected expressly to defeat the new law. Then, again, they had to contend with the easily aroused popular dislike of centralized administration, reinforced by the still more easily roused popular sentiment against severity of treatment. Expressions such as these, "Bashaws of Somerset House," "unconstitutional," "tyrannical," "dictatorship," "star-chamber," "concentrated icicles," were heard at every electioneering meeting, and it became evident that the Commissioners would have to fight hard for their existence.

This they did in the Report of 1839, to which previous reference has been made, and which, dictated and inspired as it was by something like temper and the spirit of resistance to blind injustice, is one of the very ablest and most decisive State papers ever written. The description they give of the duties and operations of the Board may serve for the present day. They distinguish between the business they originate and that which arises out of the applications for advice by the local authorities. The first consists of the introduction and maintenance of the machinery of the Poor Law, such as the constitution of unions, election of guardians, defining the duties of officers, restrictions upon out-relief, survey and valuation of rateable property. The second con-

---

[1] A report from Devonshire states that the people were taught to believe that the bread given in relief was poisoned, in order to kill the paupers off, and was in consequence rejected with horror.

[2] *Edinburgh Review*, No. 149 (attributed to Mr. Nassau Senior)

sists in dealing with all the difficult, especially legal,
questions which the novelty of the law was sure to raise.
And they point out that centralization was inevitable in
all branches of national administration, and was particularly needed in a department where so many gross evils,
that had grown up for want of it, had been but just
partially extirpated, and would be sure to break forth if
once the strong hand of the Commission was removed.
They further pointed out that a Central Board took the
responsibility and bore the blame of proceedings which,
however right and just, the local authorities could not be
expected to carry out if left to face the force of public
opinion by themselves; and also that they relieved
Parliament of the burden and unpopularity of issuing
detailed regulations in order to promulgate and carry
into effect the laws which Parliament had enacted. The
defence so far succeeded that the Commission was re-
newed annually for three successive years, and in 1842
was established for five years more.

At the close of this period in 1847 a change was
made which was warranted by the circumstances of the
times. The special reforming functions of the Commission, as a body standing aloof from Parliament and
from politics, had now been discharged, and it was
thought advisable that a ministerial department should
be constituted responsible to Parliament, and able to
defend itself where it was attacked. Accordingly several
of the chief officers of State were named Commissioners
for administering the Poor Law, together with a person
or persons specially nominated by the Crown, the
responsible minister being called the President of the
Poor Law Board. Twenty years afterwards it began to

be felt that Poor Law administration had come to be a comparatively simple matter, and that under any circumstances it hardly required a separate department for itself. Added to this there was the growing necessity of making some provision, in rural places especially, for a revival of local government, in connection with such matters as the public health and primary education. In 1871, therefore, the name of the department was altered into the Local Government Board, which was placed more entirely under one responsible head by the other Cabinet Ministers ceasing to be *ex officio* members of it, and in that capacity to countersign the documents which it issued. But whether as regards the central or the local authorities, it is only as far as concerns the administration of the Poor Law that they belong to the subject of this book.

Now, it is to the Central Board, by whatever name it has been known, that every iota of the organization we are about to describe is directly due. From first to last the Poor Law has been exactly what the Poor Law Board has made it, and there has been no relaxation of the absolute control which the Board has exercised over every detail of administration. It will be of interest, therefore, to point out the means by which this control has been exercised and maintained.

To begin with, there is the power to issue orders and rules in order to carry out the intentions of the Legislature, in respect of which the largest latitude was allowed by the Poor Law Amendment Act. No Union could be formed, nor workhouse built, nor mode of giving relief adopted, except by authority of the Commissioners. Setting aside the letters of instruction, which are rather

of the nature of explanations and suggestions, the actual
orders now in force—themselves in many cases only con-
solidations of numerous earlier regulations which they
have superseded—occupy many hundred pages of printed
matter, and extend over the whole field of administration down to the smallest details that can be imagined.
A very effective instrument of control is to be found in
the almost innumerable forms or schedules according to
which not only are all returns to be made, but all the business of relief to be transacted. It is not possible, indeed,
to move a single step without using them. Those relating
to the smallest matters that have come under my notice
are instructions how to make tea and rice puddings.

The most important orders are those of 1844, for-
bidding relief to the able-bodied, called the General Prohibitory Order; the Consolidated Order of 1847, laying
down strict regulations for (amongst other things) the
meetings of guardians, the management of workhouses,
and the duties of officers; another in 1867, regulating the
mode of keeping accounts; and another as to vagrancy in
1871. What, then, we naturally ask is the machinery by
which obedience to these orders is peremptorily enforced?

First there are the Inspectors, who in 1847 took the
place of Assistant Commissioners. These gentlemen have
been called the eyes and ears of the Board, and the reports
which they present to their department, some of which
are published in the annual Blue Book, are often of a
value far beyond the immediate occasion which calls
them forth. They are not only interesting expositions
of Poor Law policy and practice, but frequently throw
much light upon curious phases of English social life and
even of our national characteristics. And whatever else

may be said of the Poor Law, it is at least true that it
has to deal with human beings, and that too in such a
way as to open up some of the most delicate and interesting questions that human nature, with all its
follies, foibles, and eccentricities, can give rise to. We
suspect that Poor Law administrators see as much
as most people of the various aspects of life, especially
of those that are either humorous or pathetic, or both
together.

The specific duties of the inspector are to attend the
meetings of Boards of Guardians, where he may take
part in the proceedings without the power of voting;
to inspect workhouses and every place where relief is
administered; to investigate complaints, should any be
made; to give advice in doubtful cases, and to bring the
results of his experience and knowledge before the local
administrators; to point out mistakes, and also the
tendencies or results of a given policy; to hint at praise
or censure in at any rate extreme cases. To enable all
this to be done the country is divided into eleven districts for purposes of inspection, whereof the South-
Eastern contains the largest number of Unions (98), and
the Metropolis the smallest (30). It is clear from this
that inspection is not intended to be of a very close and
scrutinizing character, which indeed is not required by
the nature of the office or the conditions of the case.

The second instrument of control possessed by the
Central Board is the power of audit. The auditor
examines the accounts of every authority and official, all
of which are drawn up according to forms provided for
the purpose, and it is his duty to refuse to pass any item
where he suspects the least transgression of the law.

To make this clear by an instance : It is a condition of
giving out-relief that children, if there be any of a
school age, should attend school; and we may observe
that until quite lately educational requirements were
stricter in the case of paupers than in that of the
ordinary public.   Before, then, the auditor will allow the
relief that has been given to A, he will require to be
shown from certificate of attendance that A's children
have duly attended school, and if none be forthcoming
he will surcharge the Guardians with the amount.   There
is then an appeal to the Central Board, where the decision
of the auditor is generally upheld, but the surcharge
remitted by the exercise of the " equitable jurisdiction "
vested in the Board.   In one year, out of 346 appeals,
the power of remission was exercised in 264 cases and
refused in 18.   But in every case the surcharge operates
as a very effective warning not to transgress again, and
brings before the notice of the Central Board any irregu-
larities that may be committed.[1]

The number of audit districts is 33, not including the
Metropolis, and they extend over one or more counties
according to size.   Within his own district the auditor
has jurisdiction over the accounts of every authority
empowered to raise money by local rating.

The third and not least effective weapon of control is
the power which the Central Board has to discharge all

---

[1] It may be mentioned that it is also the auditor's duty to
ascertain whether there is any undue waste of articles of food or
drink, and that calculations have been made to enable him to
know for how much waste he should allow.   As a curiosity of legal
interpretation we may add that it has been solemnly decided that
he need not put his pen through the disallowed item, but merely
write that word against it.—(See Glen's *Poor Law Orders*, p. 592.)

officials employed by the local authorities, who in turn
may not discharge their servants without the permission
of the Board. The natural and intended effect of this is
to make the officers virtually independent of the Local
Boards so long as they do their duty, and to prevent
pressure being put upon them to evade the directions of
the department. The inspector is expected to interfere
with any unfair treatment of a zealous officer, or unworthy partiality for an incompetent one; and no officer
can be dismissed even for gross misconduct without, if
he asks for it, an investigation conducted by an inspector
according to the forms of a trial at law.

It is impossible not to see that the system just described constitutes a form of centralized administration
as strong as could well be imagined. It is true that it
may be defended, as the Report of 1839 did defend it,
by a reference to other departments, such as the Army,
the Treasury, and Primary Education. But the parallel
does not hold altogether good. For in other cases the
departments have to deal either with men who are their
own servants, or more commonly with men, *e.g.* soldiers
and teachers, whose business it is to discharge, under
general regulations, certain professional duties of which
they alone have a special and technical knowledge, and
for which they receive payment from the State. But
the local authorities or Guardians are unpaid, and are
elected by their constituencies to exercise functions which
are supposed to require deliberation, and involve responsibility. Hence it is clear that one of two things must
happen : Either the local administration of the Poor
Law will cease to have any interest or attraction for the
men who are most competent to preside over it, or else

the men elected to serve upon it will find out for themselves some opportunity of exercising a discretion of their
own. What has been the actual course of events we are
now to see.

PART II.—THE LOCAL AUTHORITIES.

One of the first duties of the Poor Law Commissioners
under the Act of 1834 was to divide the country into
districts, for the purposes of local administration. The
obvious plan was adopted of making the larger towns,
with their suburbs, into separate districts, and also dealing the same way with old country parishes, *e.g.* Wolstan-
ton, wherever they extended over a large area and
contained a sufficient population. In the case of rural
places, parishes to the number of upon an average from
twenty to thirty were grouped round the nearest market
town, whence came the name Union, as applied to all
the districts alike. This, which ought to have been a
comparatively easy task, was much impeded, not only by
local jealousies and disagreements, but by one of those
causes which no country but England would tolerate, and
which seem to savour of that incurable pedantry that
some of our critics are wont to charge us with. Previous
to the passing of the Act of 1834 we have noticed that
voluntary Unions had been formed, called, from the author
of the Act, Gilbert Incorporations, and consisting of just
such parishes as, without any regard to convenience of
locality, had chosen to unite together. And as, in spite
of reiterated demands from the Central Board, Parliament
refused to give it leave to dissolve these incorporations
except with their own consent, it became frequently very

difficult to arrange the Unions on a convenient system.[1]
But these difficulties have long been overcome, and all
England is now divided into 647 Unions, fresh ones
being formed every now and then, as new centres of
population are created; sometimes, on the other hand, two
adjacent Unions are thrown together. Thirty of these are
in the Metropolis, each of the large old parishes forming
one. The eastern counties, more especially Lincolnshire,
would seem to contain Unions with the largest number
of parishes, rising in several cases to considerably over
fifty. And Lincoln itself would head the list with 99
parishes, but for one of those survivals that are so pictur-
esque in English history, by which the City of London,
probably the smallest Union in actual extent, is credited
with no less than 112 separate parishes.

Each of the parishes in the Union, or of the wards in
large towns, elects one representative or more, according
to population, to the Union Board, of which magistrates
are *ex officio* members, though they rarely attend. But
our business lies with the Guardian only regarded as an
administrator of relief, and we must follow him at once
into the Board-room at the workhouse, outside of which
he is a mere private person, and has no separate or personal
duties whatsoever. Thus the duty of collecting rates and
of giving relief in cases of extreme urgency are fragments
of his old power still retained by the overseer, being
viewed in the latter case by the Guardians with a jealousy

[1] Most of the old incorporations have been dissolved, but some
remain, with evil effects that are felt to this day. Thus the largest
and wealthiest new suburb of Oxford is separated from the rest of
the city and joined to a rural Union for no other reason than that
the city is an incorporation, and seems for some inscrutable reason
unwilling to surrender the name.

so marked that it is very rarely exercised. But within the walls of the Board room all the poor relief of the district passes at any rate through the Guardians' hands, and every effort is made by the Central Board to impress them with the sense of the reality of the powers they exercise, and of their responsibility for the proper performance of delicate and important duties. In order to gain some idea of the spirit which is supposed to animate the local authorities, and which may be thought of more importance than the details of administration, let us gather the following description of their duties from a report of 1846, together with that of 1839.[1]

"When the Board of Guardians is once in operation its powers are very extensive; it dispenses all relief, appoints all paid officers, and administers all other Poor Law business in the Union, subject only to the general superintendence of the Commissioners and to the regulations issued by them." "The Board of Guardians forms an important and highly respectable representative body, being elected by the most numerous constituency known to the law." "We have ever sought to exercise our powers in such a manner as to avoid all unnecessary interference with Boards of Guardians, and have carefully abstained from doing anything which might extinguish the spirit of local independence." "For such local abuses as may occur the Boards of Guardians are in general primarily responsible. They have the chief part of the local power, and must therefore bear the chief part of the local responsibility." "The Commissioners (1846) state their conviction, derived from experience, of the generally

---

[1] The report of 1846 is practically a reproduction at greater length of that of 1839, and is given by Nicholls, vol. ii. p. 402, etc. etc.

discreet, trustworthy, attentive, and considerate manner
in which the Boards of Guardians discharge their functions, and of their readiness to devote to the transaction
of the business as much of their time as can be reason-
ably expected of the unpaid members of a body so
constituted."

The above describes fairly enough the intentions of
the Legislature and of the department that carries them
into effect; but facts are stronger than intentions, and
it remains to be seen how far, as a matter of fact,—especially now that the administration of relief has long got
over the first difficulties and experiments,—the purely
Poor Law duties of Guardians [1] deserve such epithets as
"important" and "responsible." Let it be remembered
that the task of superintending officers in the discharge
of duties regulated down to the most minute particulars
by superior authority, important as it is, does not involve
the KIND of importance that is usually associated with
elected bodies. Men are chosen to deliberate and discuss, and deliberation implies discretion, which, again, con-
fers responsibility. Suppose, then, a Guardian elected
after a hot contest by a large number of votes, going
every week or fortnight a journey of perhaps several
miles to the place of meeting at the expense of much
valuable time, what subjects will he find when he gets
there that will exercise his faculty of discretion? We
will try and make the answer clear.

He will, in the first instance, be struck with the fact

---

[1] It must be remembered that we are speaking of Guardians only
as administrators of Poor Law. The duties that have been of late
imposed upon them in connection with public health, education,
and (if they choose) the management of the roads, constitute a
very important addition indeed to their original functions.

that the power possessed by every representative assembly
of regulating its own proceedings within the limits of
custom or common law is not possessed by the Guardians,
but is regulated by sixteen articles which define the
duties of the Board as to its way of transacting business.
These include the times of meeting, appointment of
presiding officers, time for adjournment in case of non-
attendance, mode of voting, and order in which the business is to be taken.   There is nothing in any of these
that calls for further notice, except that the position of
the clerk, being, as he is, irremovable by the Local Board,
and answerable to the Board above for the correctness of
an immense number of details, legal questions included,
gives him a supremacy much greater than is usually held
by similar officers.   Then next he will discover that a
good deal of the Poor Law business proper is administered
by committees whose duties, again, are often of a formal
character.   Thus a man may be Guardian for many years
without seeing the interior of the house, and a member
of the Visiting Committee without doing more than pay
an occasional formal visit.   There is a Finance Committee,
but so intricate and difficult are the accounts that the
clerk is here practically supreme.   (Of course this very
general description must be taken as subject to many
variations, and in large towns there is no doubt more to
be done by action of the Guardians themselves.)   Passing
over such minor matters as examining and accepting
tenders for goods (as regulated by eight articles in the
Order of 1847), we now come to the only responsible
part of a Guardian's duties.   "They shall hear and consider any applications for relief which may be then made,
and determine thereon."

It is understood that the Guardians must admit every applicant to a personal hearing, the application having been first made to the relieving officer, about whom hereafter.[1] But it is very doubtful whether the Board (or the Relief Committee, should one be appointed) would be justified in refusing indoor relief to any applicant who insisted upon admission. An instructional letter of 1842 lays it down that the power of discharging from the workhouse should only be exercised in cases where the pauper could be proceeded against criminally for neglecting to maintain his family; and the reason assigned "that persons not really destitute will not be willing to remain in the house" covers the case of those who are willing to enter it. Practically, therefore, this set of cases settle themselves. Then, supposing out-relief to be decided upon, the amount and duration of this, even in the most irregularly managed Boards, is generally roughly settled by some standard, and does not call for much serious discussion. There remains, therefore, one solitary question of the very deepest practical importance both to the working of the Poor Law and the welfare of the labouring classes generally, namely, whether the relief given shall be indoor or outdoor. Here the Guardians have, within certain limits, a very absolute discretion indeed, and it is the deciding between different opinions and policies in respect of the kind of relief to be offered that makes the duties of Guardians interesting to themselves and to their constituents. What that discretion is,

[1] It has been held that any person not having the means of providing food for his children, and delaying to apply for relief so long that death ensued, is guilty of manslaughter.—(Glen, *Poor Law Orders*, p. 69.)

and how they have used it, we will now consider under
the head of out-relief : it is of the very essence of our
subject.

PART III.—OUT-RELIEF.

The reader will remember that (to quote once more
the Report of 1839) "the fundamental principle with
respect to legal relief is that the condition of the pauper
ought to be, on the whole, less eligible than that of the
independent labourer ;" and he will agree with the same
report in the assertion "that all distribution of relief in
money or in goods, to be spent or consumed by the
pauper in his own house, is inconsistent with the principle
in question." Accordingly the first object of the Poor
Law Commissioners was to put a stop to out-relief.
Beginning in their first year with two districts, namely,
Cookham Union and Sandridge Parish (First Report,
page 28), they proceeded gradually in the face of much
opposition,[1] till in the year 1844 a final order (reproducing one of 1839), called the Outdoor Prohibitory
Relief Order, was issued, in which it was laid down that
"every able-bodied person . . . requiring relief . . .
shall be relieved only in the workhouse of the Union,"
etc. In the face of which order we are confronted with
the fact that in the beginning of this year (1881) the
number of *adult able-bodied* outdoor paupers was returned
for the 1st of January at 84,812, while indoor paupers

---

[1] The opposition was chiefly in respect of allowances to large
families, to retain which every effort was made. Also the indoor
test system was severely tried by stagnation of trade at Nottingham,
Andover, and other places. Nor could it be applied until the
Houses were ready.

were only 26,357, *i.e.* of the same class.   And again, of the
268,923 outdoor paupers returned as adult not able-bodied,
by far the larger number were persons whom only the
approach of age (after sixty paupers are treated as not
able-bodied) had rendered destitute after a life of ability
to do work.   What is the explanation of this apparent
anomaly?

It is this.   The Report of 1839 states that the Commissioners "permit out-relief to the able-bodied *in all
those cases of distress which are of most frequent occurrence,
such as sickness, accident, bodily or mental infirmity in themselves and in their families.*"   This exception is carried
forward into the General Prohibitory Order, and is increased by the addition of such cases as burial, widow-
hood for six months after the death of the husband, and
for so long as there is any child dependent on the widow.
Now from this two facts are clear.   First, inasmuch as persons above sixty are not to be considered necessarily able-
bodied, and are therefore outside the terms of the order,
all aged persons who have made no provision for themselves during middle life may receive out-relief if the
Guardians resolve to grant it.   And secondly, all persons
under sixty, if disabled by any cause either in their own
persons or that of any of their families, are also eligible
for the same kind of relief.   Now, it has been stated (see
page 15) that the two chief evils to which poor relief
gives rise are idleness on the part of those who can work
and will not, and improvidence on the part of those who
can make provision for possible sickness or inevitable
old age, but prefer to trust to the bounty of the State.
The first class was dealt with finally and summarily in
the Prohibitory Order, which forbids relief to any man

capable of earning wages. But the second was by the
express exceptions contained in that order left to the
discretion of the local authorities, who have not been
slow to avail themselves of the opportunity. How far
the central authorities realized that this departure from
their own admitted principles would lead once more to
the establishment of a gigantic system of pauperism,
in which the unthrifty and careless were maintained
at the cost or to the prejudice of their more provident
neighbours, does not very clearly appear. Certain
it is that it has been turned by local administration
to this end, and that, too, in spite of warnings almost
amounting to threats, and expostulations almost descending to entreaties, from the Poor Law authorities themselves.

In saying this there is no intention to impute blame
in any quarter, which would be in every way unseemly.
But our object is to give such an account of the working
of the Poor Law as shall convey to the reader some
notion of the spirit in which it is administered, and also
explain the tendencies that have led to the results actually
before us. We shall therefore trace the operation of
the law of out-relief somewhat more in detail.

The functionary through whom the Guardians perform
this part of their work is that well-known person, the
relieving officer, whose duties are prescribed in fifteen sections of Article 215 of the General Consolidated Order of
1847 (Glen, p. 215). The one that concerns us at present
is No. 2, which states that he shall receive "all applications for relief made to him within his district, and
forthwith examine into the circumstances of every case
by visiting the house of the applicant, and by making all

necessary inquiries, etc. etc., and report the result of such
inquiries in the prescribed form at the next meeting."
The "prescribed form" is called the Application and
Report Book, and contains headings for all information
that may be useful to the Guardians, including one that
is much neglected, showing "names of relations liable by
law to relieve the applicant" (see Report by Mr. Sendall,
1874, and Mr. Wodehouse, 1872).   This book is laid
before the chairman for him to record the decision of the
Guardians at the "Board Day," whither the applicant is
also summoned to attend, and be further questioned as
to his destitution.   But from the beginning to the end
of this procedure one remark holds good : that unlimited
discretion leads to unlimited variation in the methods by
which it is carried out.   Thus, the number of relieving
officers in proportion to population and area varies in-
definitely.   One officer had 400 cases under his charge,
the usual number being 200 to 250.   Again, the practice
of requiring the personal attendance of the applicant at
the Board varies considerably, a man being always anxious
to put it off upon his wife, and a woman upon some fair-
spoken neighbour, while in some cases quite young girls
are sent to plead the cause of their destitute relatives.
The attendance of the Guardians themselves is of course
fluctuating, and the fate of the applicants,—that is to say,
whether they shall submit to a species of imprisonment
or enjoy a little pension at their own homes,—not unfre-
quently depends upon whether this or that Guardian
(the chairman especially) chances to be present or absent.
In some Unions where there is a Relief Committee, one
man (though it is believed that three are necessary to
make a quorum in order to grant relief legally) some-

times adjudicates upon all the cases, and he, again, may be a strenuous supporter of the workhouse test one day, and an equally strong advocate for out-relief the next. Then, again, the time allowed for the disposal of each case at all times too short, is by no means the same, varying, according to the experience of one inspector (see Mr. Longley's Report on Out-Relief in the Metropolis, 1873), from eleven cases in four minutes to three minutes for each case. And there is an absolutely concurrent testimony that there neither is nor can be anything like adequate information as to the circumstances of the case upon which the Guardians can base their decision. But the subject of investigation deserves a special word of notice.

The plain fact is that the workhouse test has *killed* the spirit of investigation, as, by the confession of its supporters, it was meant to do. The following is quoted from the Report of 1839 :—"The only sure mode of ascertaining whether the total receipts of the labourer" (for this in the case before us we should read "total sources of income") "are really sufficient is to offer in lieu of them an adequate but less eligible maintenance, which will not be accepted unless necessity requires it. This can be effected by the offer of the workhouse, and by that only." Having this to fall back on in all doubtful cases, both relieving officers and Guardians are under strong inducement to dispense with long, costly, and disagreeable enquiries. The former pays his one preliminary visit (sometimes in large towns carefully prepared for by removal of furniture), and gathers just as much as local gossip can tell him. The latter have no means of knowing the facts of the case except what they can wring

in a hurried cross-examination from some unfortunate
applicant,—in nothing more unfortunate than this, that
he is driven to gain his ends by craft and concealment,—
more especially as to whether his friends can keep him,
or as to what he receives from charity.   But at this
point ensues a curious phenomenon.   Though Guardians
are practically powerless in many cases to ascertain the
reality of that destitution *which is the only legal title to
relief,* yet they do know something about the character of
the applicant, which, if the plain truth must be told, has
nothing to do with it.[1]   Thus if two men under precisely
the same circumstances apply for relief, one of whom has
borne a good character and succumbed to misfortune, the
other has been just the reverse, it is still not permissible,
upon any sound principle of Poor Law, to make a difference between them.   And if we attend to the matter for
a moment we shall see that the attempt to pass a moral
judgment upon the two, involving the most serious
material consequences, would necessitate, to be fair, a
preliminary enquiry into their education, home influences,
conduct of children, natural temperament, and the opportunities each had enjoyed of getting on in life.   No
doubt the temptation to exercise a moral discrimination
is irresistible, and the Guardians try, with probably some
success, to achieve a rough and ready justice, of which it
may be said that it is morally excellent, but it is not Poor
Law.

These, then, are the practical difficulties under which

[1] The Poor Law Board stated in answer to a direct question in
1870 that, "according to strict law," if there were two widows,
each requiring ten shillings per week, one of whom received four
shillings from a club, the Guardians must allow her only six shillings and the other ten.—(Glen, p. 63.)

the Guardians meet to exercise their discretion as to
whether indoor or out-relief shall be given. But, and this
is commonly the decisive argument, it is cheaper to allow
a weekly pittance outside the house than to give main
tenance within it—cheaper, that is, in any given case,
though not in the long run, for all experience shows that
the persistent refusal of out-relief does not increase the
inmates of the house.   But after all there is something
stronger than even this. The Guardians know that every
applicant who stands before them has been encouraged
by the law to expect some allowance of out-relief whenever
age or sickness has rendered him destitute. Is it reasonable to expect that they will, as a rule, take upon themselves the disagreeable responsibility of refusing the relief
which the law allows them to give? If the Central Board
or the Legislature, who are removed from actual contact
with the pleadings of destitution, perhaps in the case of
old workmen or even friends, shrink from prohibiting out-
relief in such cases, how can the Guardians, with natural
benevolence to prompt them and a character for kindness
to keep up, abstain from following the easy course that
saves them further trouble, and satisfies the conscience
(until aroused by argument) and the pocket (until convinced by statistics and results) as well. The result is that
the discretion enjoyed by Guardians tends steadily, though
with very wide variations, in one direction, and that
out-relief becomes the rule, indoor relief the exception.
The proportion, excluding vagrants and lunatics, may be
stated now at about one indoor pauper to 3.2 outdoor;
ten years ago the proportion was one indoor to nearly six
outdoor.   There has therefore been some improvement in
deference to the pressure of the Central Board and the

moie enlightened opinion of some Poor Law reformers.
But enough remains to show that while the new Poor
Law has dealt satisfactorily with the case of those who
preferred to seek relief rather than work for wages (at
worst a case so abnormal and unnatural that there could
be no real difficulty in grappling with it), it has failed to
meet the case of those who prefer relying upon relief to
making provision against destitution out of their own
resources.   One half the work has been done, the other
half,—including also the natural call upon relations,
friends, and charity to "maintain their own poor"—is
yet to be begun.

We have, however, hitherto only traced the system of
out-relief up to the moment when it is first given to the
applicant by the Guardians: we have now to carry our
description to the mode in which it is distributed and
continued.

That part of relief (by far the most important) which
consists in grants of a certain weekly allowance to the
sick and infirm is distributed by the relieving officer, who
attends periodically at stated times and places (in country
places once every week), in accordance with the regulation that orders him "duly and punctually to supply
the weekly allowances of all paupers belonging to his
district." This may be given in money or in kind, and
it is thought that the principle of poor relief is best carried
out by the latter system.   But in practice the giving of
money is found so much more convenient, and the argument, that if people are to have relief at all they had
better be left to make the best of it for themselves, seems
so reasonable that relief in kind has become the exception.   The book in which the paupers of each parish are

entered is a very elaborate affair, containing no less than twenty-five different classes to which the recipient may belong. It is examined by the clerk and auditor, and forms the basis upon which the statistics of pauperism are framed. It is also the duty of the relieving officer to keep a strict supervision over the recipients of relief, and report to the Guardians such change in their circumstances as may have occurred, especially when the time expires for which their relief was granted, or for that periodical revision of the list of paupers which is carefully carried out by every properly-conducted Board.

Besides this there are, however, two other modes of giving out-relief. First it may be given to the able-bodied in some Unions in return for labour, in which case half of it must be in kind, and the work done under the superintendence of a special officer appointed for that purpose : the labour is mostly in the stoneyard. About 120 Unions, including the Metropolis and the larger towns, are allowed to employ this labour test instead of the house test, and are therefore not under the Outdoor Relief Prohibitory Order, but under the Outdoor Relief Regulation Order of December 1852. The reason of this policy is contained in a letter of 1852, in which the Board draws attention to "the circumstances of most of the Unions and parishes in London, and in some other populous places," in consequence of which they "leave the Guardians at liberty to offer relief in the workhouse only," but " do not prohibit out-relief to any class of paupers." The outdoor labour test would seem, then, to be reserved for special cases, as a "safety valve" at a time of great and sudden depression of trade. But it does not seem to be very extensively used, and is growing more and more unpopular with the relieving authorities.

The other form of out-relief is the medical. The whole of England is divided into districts which may not exceed 15,000 acres in extent, or 15,000 persons in population, and are in practice much smaller. Over each of these the Guardians appoint a medical officer residing in the district, who must, according to the regulations, "attend duly and punctually upon all poor persons requiring medical attendance, and supply the requisite medicines whenever he may be lawfully required by an order of the Guardians, or of a relieving officer, or of an overseer." He is bound to attend under such an order even when he may know that the person is not indigent, but he can report the circumstances at the next meeting. He cannot order articles of food for a sick pauper, but he can recommend them; and practically Guardians naturally shrink from the responsibility of refusing what he suggests. Persons already paupers are not relieved by special order, but receive a ticket, upon the exhibition of which the medical officer is bound to attend to them. He must give the Guardians such information as they may require, and must make a return of days on which visits were paid or attendance given, together with an account of the patients' condition. Medical relief given to parents alone does not make the children paupers.

Such are the arrangements whereby out-relief is granted and distributed: How, is the next natural enquiry, does the system work in actual operation? To answer this question we must refer to an enormous mass of literature, known as the reports of the inspectors who have from time to time been appointed to examine the

out-relief system for the instruction of the Central
Board.[1]

A careful examination of these reports (or some of
them) will show that there is an absolute concurrence as to
two main features in the working of outdoor relief.   In
the first place, considering that the reformed Poor Law
was expressly intended to introduce uniformity and
system, it has to be confessed that in this respect the
failure is very great indeed.   The exercise of local discretion has led to an almost infinite variableness of administration.   No two Unions have the same principles
or rules for dealing with the same class of cases; no two
officers take the same views as to the nature of their
duties or the best way of performing them; and, what
is worse, no two destitute persons under similar circumstances can be at all sure of being dealt with in the same
way.   A kind of moral uncertainty is thus cast over the
minds of the "poor," which, with its accompanying
results of jealousy, disappointment, sense of injustice,
and gambling away life upon the chance of out-relief,
probably inflicts as much injury upon their mental, as
the old system did upon their material, comfort.—(See
Mr. Longley's Report, p. 30.)

In the next place, the reports are perfectly unanimous
in their testimony as to the prevailing ignorance concerning
the "cases" upon which the Guardians have to adjudicate.
" The main reliance of Guardians must be placed in the
regular and *unintermitting* routine of enquiry pursued by

---

[1] The public is little aware of the ability, industry, and minute
thoroughness which characterize these and other reports on Poor
Law administration.   May it not well be that such a system as
outdoor relief absorbs more than its share of these qualities ?

paid and responsible officers." " I cannot but think that a much nearer approach to it than is now made is possible." —(Mr. Wodehouse, p. 37.)   " I detected considerable irregularity in the strict performance by the relieving officers of these all-important duties."—(Mr. Henley, *Annual Report of Poor Law Board for* 1871, p. 96.)   But perhaps the following story, told by Mr. Sendall (p. 7), will serve to show to what extent out-relief may be abused from lack of information : it is but one out of hundreds upon hundreds that are mentioned in the reports, and which are practically known to exist throughout the country:—

"One of the officers of the —— Union, engaged shortly after his appointment in looking up his cases, came upon a pauper of long standing at work in a well-stocked garden.

" ' You have got a nice bit of garden here ? '

" ' Yes ; it is pretty good.'

" ' And are those your pigs in the sty there ? '

" ' Yes ; they be mine.'

" ' And there is a horse and cart—is that yours too ? '

" ' Oh, yes ; that is what I goes to market with.   And who be you, sir ? '

" ' Well, I am the new relieving officer ; and I think you had better come up and see the Guardians at next Board day.' " [1]

After this we need not be surprised to hear the stories of paupers dying rich.

We shall next attempt to condense the defects noted

[1] The possibility of the existence of such cases is part of the price the nation pays for the destruction of municipal self-government in country places.

by the inspectors as proceeding from the want of uniformity and of information. We take the following
twelve points more for the sake of the round number
than for any hope of exhausting the list :—

(1.) The attendance of Guardians being fluctuating,
and the composition of the Board on any one day uncertain, makes them what one inspector terms "pliable,"
especially in the way of yielding to the applicant's persistent refusal to enter the house. There is also a
marked tendency to compromise cases by small temporary
doles, and at times to evade the law in doing so.[1]

(2.) The revision of the lists of paupers by the
Guardians is very irregular. In some it is done punctually every quarter; in others at chance times; in some
once a year, or even once in three years. The consequence is that in cases where destitution has ceased
pauperism remains. As the visits of the relieving
officers are mainly determined by the practice of the
Guardians in respect of revising, it follows that the visits
are at most uncertain intervals.

(3.) There is great laxity as to requiring the personal
attendance of applicants. It is in many cases dispensed
with; and the Guardians rely on the information of the
relieving officer, and the opinion of the Guardian of the
parish, if present. The temptation to take the chance
of obtaining relief, and so to apply for it, is thereby
increased.

(4.) The system of the " pay table " is severely

---

[1] In illustration of this, Mr. Longley tells a story (Report, p. 66)
of the chairman who, when warned by him that some allowance of
relief was illegal, observed with great good humour that " he did
not care a pin for the inspector nor for the auditor either."

criticised. The relieving officer meets the paupers at some fixed place—sometimes even a public-house, sometimes a cottage for which rent is paid—and there distributes the relief as though he were paying wages. Children or neighbours are sent (and paid) by the pauper to receive it. The districts are so large that this plan cannot be avoided, and some Unions are obliged to pay for conveyances.[1]

(5.) There is a general complaint that the books and returns are not always accurately kept. This is of special importance in respect of classification of paupers.

(6.) The practice as to relief of deserted wives with children varies very much. No competent authority doubts that refusal of out-relief in these cases is the only course consistent with the due administration of the Poor Law. But in many cases it is given, except where the Guardians suspect "collusion." The room thus given for fraud is obvious, and complaints of fraud are common.

(7.) The case of widows with more than one child dependent upon them (they are supposed to be able to maintain one child), as it is one of the most perplexing, so is it sure to lead to difference of treatment, and thence to abuses. "General sympathy for widows has suggested a lax administration of relief" is a heading to one report. —(Mr. Longley, p. 49.) A belief is still prevalent that "to put on the cap" entitles to parish pay.—(*Ibid.* p. 50.) There is always great difficulty in discovering their earnings, and all relief must be in their case relief in aid of

---

[1] Is it really quite impossible that the overseers or some local authority should be trusted with the mere payment of relief, and so all this labour avoided ?

K

wages, with the direct result that the wages of widows
fall below that of independent women. In some cases
where the relief has been discontinued, owing to the
birth of an illegitimate child, the woman has never been
obliged to accept the house, but has maintained herself
without difficulty.   The subject is far too long and difficult for discussion here; but the reader sufficiently
interested in the matter is referred to Mr. Longley's
Report on Poor Law Administration in London (1873),
where it is fully gone into.

(8.) A very painful result of the present system is
pointed out in the fact that paupers marry paupers, or
have large families after becoming paupers, and live in
the extreme of want in consequence.   "Households
such as these are the forcing-beds of pauperism."—(Mr.
Sendall, p. 10.)

(9.) Relief is still given in aid of wages where aged
or infirm people can earn a little, or are expected to do
so.   This is unavoidable, and perhaps not very injurious,
though a contravention of all sound principles.

(10.) There is a melancholy concurrence of opinion
that relations are not called upon to help as they ought
to be, and that innumerable cases of pauperism exist
where there are relations perfectly able to help, and who
would do so (as in some cases they have done) sooner than
allow their friends to go into the house.   To take one
instance out of many, a pauper in receipt of 2s. 6d
weekly was found acting as servant in her sister's house
hold, whose position was that of a superior artizan.
Prosecutions are rare; but in many cases it is said that
the threat is sufficient.   But this can only apply in
cases where the relation is known.

(11.) Undue facilities are said to exist for receiving
medical relief, and an injurious notion has got abroad
that this kind of relief has not the same pauperizing
effects.　Very frequently the receipt of medical relief
is the beginning of pauperism, and a fear is even expressed lest the system degenerate into one of medical
State charity.　Connected with this are very grave complaints as to " medical extras," by means of which the
doctor orders food instead of medicine.　The Guardians
are then able to give relief in aid of wages, and persons are
encouraged to apply for medical relief in the hope that
food and stimulants will follow.　It happens, too, that
meat ordered for the sick is used for food for the family ;
thus " beef ordered for beef-tea to a dying husband was
found two hours later in the frying-pan."

(12.) The outdoor labour test is subject to great
abuses.　The stoneyard has an attraction for the indolent, and some cases are known in which men work at
their own employment in the summer, and " for the
Guardians," i.e. at the stoneyard, in the winter.

We trust the reader will pardon these details of de-
fective administration which have been laid before him
in order that he may know the actual working of the
system which is supported by his money, and is main-
tainable only so long as public opinion chooses to abide
by it.　Many improvements have been suggested, with
the bare mention of which we must be content.　Some
place reliance upon improved methods of administration
by local authorities.　Others would introduce a new
classification of recipients of out-relief, by which persons
of bad character (we venture to think an impossible sug-
gestion), or those whose wages have previously enabled

them to make provision for their wants, should be de-
barred from out-relief. Others, again, would make the
area of out-maintenance and administration much smaller
than that for indoor, so as to put pressure upon localis-
ties to prefer the latter, and also to subject the applicant
or the pauper to much closer supervision and control.
Others, among whom the author may perhaps be permitted to include himself, are absolutely convinced that
the whole system of out-relief could be without difficulty
abolished in a very few years, just as the old system was
abolished some forty years ago by the action of the
Central Board in issuing prohibitory orders. The conditions of the two cases seem fairly parallel.

PART IV.—INDOOR RELIEF.

The indoor relief, as established by English Poor Law,
is, we may say at once, though not without blots, as we
shall see, thoroughly worthy of the good sense and
practical humanity of the English people. With the
exception of lunatic asylums, infirmaries, and district
schools in large (mostly metropolitan) Unions, this
kind of relief is given in houses miscalled workhouses,
one of which has been built in each Union since the Act
of 1834. The name Workhouse was given them from
some idea that they would be used for the purpose of
setting able-bodied paupers to work, according to the
statute of Queen Elizabeth and the requirements of the
house test. But that test has proved so efficacious that
the number of inmates really able-bodied is comparatively
few, and the house has become the permanent home of

persons disabled by some misfortune or other from taking care of themselves. As the number of persons for whom the State thus provides a home was at the beginning of this year 189,438 (not including vagrants), and as the number is subject to constant loss and as constant renewal, so that the total passing through the house on the way to the grave is very considerable, it becomes every citizen to have some idea of the kind of institution which the law provides at his cost for the care of those who are "the poor in very deed."

We will first of all take a glance at the officers. These are the doctor, master and matron, chaplain, schoolmaster, nurse, porter, and such assistants as the size of the house renders necessary: the duties of all these are defined in the most careful manner in the order of 1847.—(Glen, pp. 182-215.)

With respect to the doctor, chaplain, and schoolmaster (or more generally mistress), no more can be said than that the professional duties which they are accustomed or expected to perform in the exercise of their respective callings elsewhere are rigorously exacted on behalf of the inmates of the house, and that any known neglect would be visited by immediate censure, to be followed by dismissal, if persisted in. Thus, to take one instance, it is not thought right to administer Holy Communion except there is a chapel set apart for divine service, but the paupers should be allowed to go to the parish church for that purpose. Permission to attend church or chapel is optional with the Guardians, and there are special provisions for allowing the attendance of ministers of religion in case any inmate desires to be

visited by a minister of his own denomination. The
conditions upon which this right should be exercised
were definitely settled in the case of the Roman Catholic
inmates of Chelsea Workhouse in 1861, under the
authority of the Court of Queen's Bench (Glen, p. 125).
It need hardly be added that the inmates are under the
protection of the "conscience clause," and that in particular the children of paupers enjoyed that protection
long before it was vouchsafed to the children of the
independent labourer.

It is, however, the master and matron upon whom it
depends whether the intentions of the Legislature are
carried out towards the unfortunate persons who have
accepted maintenance from the State, and neither regulations nor such supervision as the Guardians can give
will avail much against the consequences of their faults
and shortcomings. No one, not even we should think
the captain of a man of war, has more absolute control
within his own domain, or can make his power more
sharply felt. Everything that careful regulations can
accomplish is done in order to make them discharge the
duties of their office properly. They are instructed to
see that every pauper upon admission (which must be
by order of the Guardians, or provisionally by the relieving officer, or in cases of emergency by the master
himself) is searched, cleansed,[1] clothed, and put in the

[1] Perhaps the following extracts from the regulations as to bath-
ing will give as good an idea as we can have of the excessive care
bestowed upon the management of the house :—"(1) Every patient
(*i.e.* lunatic) must be bathed once a week unless exempted by medical order ; (3) The cold water is always to be turned on first ; (4)
Temperature must not be less than 88 or more than 98 degrees, and
must be suspended at once if the thermometer is out of order ; (8)

proper ward. They must enforce order, industry, punctuality, and cleanliness. They must read prayers morning and evening. They must enforce employment upon every inmate according to his or her capacity for work, and allow no one who can work to be idle at any time. They must visit the wards (the master or matron, according to the sex of the occupants) every morning at eleven to see that they are duly cleansed, and every night in summer at ten and in winter at nine to see that the paupers are in bed. They are to take care that no pauper, upon the approach of death, is left unattended night or day, and to give notice of his death to the nearest relations who may be known to exist. Lastly, they are to say or cause to be said grace before and after meals.

The duties of the porter require a special word of mention, because that officer is the outward symbol, so to speak, of that Poor Law constraint which may be defined as voluntary imprisonment. He is to keep the gate and allow no one to go in or out without leave of the master, except of course the Poor Law officers. He is further to register the names and business of every person visiting the house, and to see that nothing unlawful is brought into it. The gates are locked at nine and opened in the morning at six.

We turn next to the government of the workhouse, as it applies to the inmates themselves, the spirit and intention of which is thus described in the Report of 1839. "The rules which we have issued are of two classes. 1. Those which are necessary to the mainte-

UNDER NO PRETENCE WHATEVER is the patient's head to be put under water."—Glen, p. 196.

nance of good order in any building in which considerable numbers of persons of both sexes and of different
ages reside. 2. Those which are necessary in order
that these establishments may not be almshouses but
workhouses in the proper meaning of the term, and may
produce the results which the Legislature intended."
This second clause points back to an old controversy,
which was at that time still unsettled. A strong disposition was evinced to modify the arrangements of the
houses, so as to make them in the case of the aged and
infirm into almshouses, against which it was urged with
irresistible force that the house would then no longer
operate as an inducement to persons to provide support
for themselves or their relatives in declining years.
Facts, however, once more are stronger than intentions,
and partly owing to the efficacy of the test, partly owing
to the giving of out-relief to the infirm and aged, the
workhouse is, as we have said, practically an infirmary
or almshouse for the worst cases of impotence and suffering. But its original conception still adheres to it, namely,
to "subject the pauper inmate to such a system of
labour, discipline, and restraint, as shall be sufficient to
outweigh in his estimation the bodily comforts which he
enjoys." This has been accomplished very effectually,
more so, it is said, in the case of the women than the
men ; but unfortunately as a means of prevention it
comes too late, for by far the larger number of those
who enter the workhouse (unless it be avowedly only for
a time) have no choice but to remain there. And the
condition does not avail to force persons to provide for
themselves in old age, because they have always the
chance of out-relief to rely on.

The methods by which this condition of steering between a jail and an almshouse, between punishment and
charity, is carried out, may be described under the heads
of classification, diet, discipline, and punishment, *i.e.* for
the unruly.　In respect of the first, the house (if properly
arranged) is divided into seven parts or wards, for as
many classes of inmates, viz. aged and infirm men, able-
bodied men, boys above seven and under fifteen, the
same three classes of women, and children under seven.
Between these there is or ought to be no communication,
and the Guardians are further empowered to subdivide
them according to their moral character or previous
habits.　It is clear, however, that this can only apply to
large houses.　There is a great number of extra regulations allowing inmates to be employed for such purposes
as nursing in other wards than their own; and as the
result of a long controversy, aged and infirm couples are
not to be separated, age receiving the rather liberal
interpretation of above sixty.[1]　And as children still
at the age of nurture, *i.e.* under seven, have a right
to be with their mother, they may be placed in the
female wards, and their mothers allowed access to them
at all reasonable times.　Above that age interviews
between parents and children must be granted once a
day.

As to food the simplest way will be to copy a dietary,
published by the Central Board, the quantities, however,
being only specimens and not absolutely binding : they
are given for men, the women being allowed in some
cases somewhat less.

---

[1] Separate apartments are sometimes provided for aged couples,
and, it is said, very seldom claimed.

	BREAKFAST		DINNER							SUPPER	
	Oatmeal Porridge.	New Milk.	Cooked Meat.	Potatoes and Vegetables.	Broth.	Bread.	Suet Pudding, with Treacle Sauce.	Soup.	Stewed Meat and Potatoes.	Porridge.	New Milk.
	Qrt.	Pt.	Oz.	Oz.	Pt.	Oz.	Oz.	Pt.	Lbs.	Qrt.	Pt.
Sunday	1	½	4	12	...	...	...	...	...	1	½
Monday	1	½	...	...	1½	7	...	..	...	1	½
Tuesday	1	½	...	...	...	...	14	½	...	1	½
Wednesday	1	½	...	...	...	6	...	1	...	1	½
Thursday	1	½	4	12	...	...	...	...	...	1	½
Friday	1	½	...	...	½	...	14	...	...	1	½
Saturday	1	½	...	...	...	...	...	...	2	1	½

The aged and infirm have, however, special allowances of tea and bread and butter, instead of porridge, for breakfast and supper, with "sugar not exceeding half an ounce to each pint of tea ;" and we may add, as curiously characteristic of the cold-blooded equity that presides over workhouse management, that an inmate can call upon the master to weigh the food provided for him in his own presence and in that of two witnesses: he can also complain to the Guardians of anything unsatisfactory in the food, with the certainty of being attentively listened to. The sick dietary is under the control of the medical officer. Lastly, as most people know, Christmas Day (together with public festivals) is the one day that is exempt from dietary regulations, and is made an occasion of regaling the inmates with a substantial repast.

In respect of discipline, the pauper inmate is never allowed to forget that he is under orders. The clothing must be such as the Guardians approve; but it is ex-

pressly forbidden to wear a distinguishing dress as a
mark of disgrace. The inmates must perform work
suitable to their capacity and without remuneration, but
privileges in the way of food are granted to persons employed in the work of the house, *e.g.* nursing. They rise
in the morning, are set to work, leave off work, meet
for meals in the common dining-room, and go to bed at
set hours, "notified by the ringing of a bell," and the
names are called over half an hour after rising. Games
of chance and smoking are prohibited, but the Guardians
are permitted and even encouraged to supply books and
newspapers. And, finally, there is a long code of regulations respecting the punishment of the two classes into
which evildoers are divided, the disorderly and the
refractory. The punishment in the first case consists
of cutting off the food according to the discretion of
the master, and of solitary confinement by order of the
Guardians for not more than twenty-four hours in the
second. Wise men will note with satisfaction that the
use of the rod is not forbidden in the case of naughty
boys, though its use is guarded by several regulations as
to the person employing it, and the time that must elapse
(two hours) after the commission of the offence. The
privilege of a flogging enjoyed by children of the upper
classes is denied to paupers above the age of fourteen.

The power of terminating this voluntary imprisonment requires to be noticed. Any pauper can leave
upon giving reasonable notice, and his family must be
sent with him, unless there are special reasons to the
contrary, such as the child being at a district school or
in the infirmary. Persons under punishment or too ill
to travel may of course be detained. Orphan children

under sixteen may be detained if the Guardians see good ground for it, above sixteen they are for Poor Law purposes considered to be of age. There is nothing to prevent the mothers of illegitimate children from discharging themselves and returning every few days. It is doubtful whether the Guardians have power to detain a wife whose husband is in the house, but they can certainly do so if the husband exercises his marital authority to forbid her departure. It results, therefore, that the pauper is perhaps the only member of the community to whom the law can afford efficient help in compelling the obedience of wives.

It is not, however, by the mere recapitulation of rules and arrangements that we can adequately describe the manner in which English Poor Law has endeavoured to carry out the principle of affording to the indigent all the necessaries of life, together with equitable and reasonable treatment, while at the same time stamping its consideration for their wants with something from which the natural man, still more the natural woman, shrinks with aversion. If the paradox may be pardoned, the spirit of a workhouse may be described as one of cheerless comfort. Much of this is quite inevitable upon any reasonable principles of Poor Law administration; much more of it belongs to the workhouse, not because it is an institution of Poor Law, but because it is an asylum for a number of persons afflicted with some of the worst evils to which flesh and spirit are heirs. But much is also due to the fact, which ought never to be lost sight of, that the workhouse has come to be something in one respect very different from what its founders expected it would be. To this point we are now to invite the reader's care-

ful attention, for it may lead us to discern the weak
parts of the present system and also the mode of improving it.　Practically, every English voter is responsible for
the treatment of some 100,000 of his fellow-countrymen,
who in the extremity of their distress have thrown
themselves upon the care of the nation; and we can
hardly overestimate the effects which their treatment
may have upon the classes from which they are mainly
drawn, upon the morality of the whole country, and upon
the conscience and spirit of the governing classes.　Upon
such a subject full information is most desirable.

The immense scale upon which the workhouses were
planned and built, and the fact that each union was to
have its own separate house, shows—first, that they were
expected to contain a large number of persons driven
into them by the want of employment; secondly, that by
their means each union was intended to discharge all the
duties it owed to all classes of its own paupers.　But as
a matter of fact (the large towns excepted) they do not
contain in many cases half, in some not a quarter of the
inmates for which they were built, so that the waste in
keeping up large unfilled establishments, each with an
expensive staff of officers, is very great indeed; thus the
salaries and rations of officers (including, however, that
proportion which is spent in the administration of out-
relief) is considerably over a million, while the total
maintenance of indoor paupers is only about a million
and three-quarters.

Again, the absence of able-bodied workers in what is
called a workhouse gives a totally different character to
the establishment.　The exceptions are not the industrious, not even the merely improvident poor, but those of

downright bad character, whom temporary pressure, perhaps of disease, has driven within its walls; the typical case is that of mothers of illegitimate children. So that a workhouse does *not* contain persons who can work, but does contain those very classes whom one would least of all select to associate with each other: both sexes, extreme ages, different degrees of imbecility and disease, those who are much to be pitied, and those who are much to be blamed. All these are under the same roof, and under the government of the same officials, who may be as fit to deal with one class of inmates as they are unfit to deal with another. Hence there comes from this aggregation of classes a something that may be described as the workhouse essence: it is neither school, infirmary, penitentiary, prison, place of shelter, or place of work, but something that comes of all these put together. Nor is it possible by any classification to prevent contact and, it may be, moral contagion; in the smaller houses classification is at all times difficult, and in no case does it hold good at meals, church, and other occasions. And it may well be that the regular and peaceable (afflicted) inmates endure much preventible suffering from the operation of this cause. [1]

[1] The most difficult case is of course that of women coming into the house to be confined, and women of bad character, who can almost come and go as they please. It may illustrate at once the difficulties of Poor Law administration and the spirit in which they are met, if we quote in connection with this subject a circular letter of the Poor Law Board (Glen, p. 103). "So long as the inmates of the workhouse conform themselves to the prescribed rules, the law does not recognize any distinction (*e.g.* as to dress or diet or time of rising) amongst them founded upon their antecedent conduct; and the Board cannot therefore sanction a particular treatment in respect of a peculiar class of inmates, which is intended to operate

But the really great sufferers by present arrangements are the children, and they are also precisely the class of paupers, the obligation to take care of whom, as being guiltless of their own destitution, presses most strongly upon the law and the nation. At present they are dealt with under one of the four following plans :—

First, The children are in by far the larger number of Unions educated by a teacher under Government inspection in the house itself—the number of children of school age being in many cases very small, and the cost therefore proportionably large. Against this plan there has never been wanting a strong and righteous protest. Thus, in the Report of 1839, Mr. Tufnell, in the course of a long argument against the practice, declares, "There is considerable danger of moral contamination to the children from their residence in the same house with adult paupers. I am confident that architectural arrangements can never secure perfect classification. Conversation is carried on over walls and through windows." He then gives other really dreadful illustrations, and concludes, "The atmosphere of a workhouse that contains adult paupers is tainted with vice; no one who regards the future happiness of the children would ever wish them to be educated within its precincts."

The curious reader will find in the Report of 1870-71 all that can be said on the other side of the question by Mr. Bowyer and Mr. Browne, two of the inspectors. But he will not, we think, be easily convinced that the

as a punishment for offences committed previous to their entrance into the workhouse. But. . . the Guardians cannot be too careful not to employ the mothers of illegitimate children in the kitchen or in domestic work generally, in which the younger and more innocent inmates of the house are engaged."

proper place for a school is a workhouse, nor will he be able to discern how it is possible not to gain both in efficiency and economy by separating the schools from the house. The good work which, in spite of disadvantages, they accomplish now would surely be increased and not lessened by such a change.

Secondly, This arrangement is modified in an increasing number of cases (at present 160) by sending the children to some neighbouring elementary school. This is a great improvement, and does something to break the unhealthy routine of workhouse life. But it is for all that a sad sight to see the children returning from school —*home*.

Thirdly, The right and sensible plan is adopted of forming district schools (at present 41) for one or more large Unions, or for educating the children in a separate building. This is the rule in the Metropolis, where the district schools are removed into the country, and there are school districts for rural Unions in Surrey and Shropshire. Besides which there are some seventy Unions (most of them in the large towns) where the return states that the children are taught in a separate building.

Fourthly, Since 1870, when the Poor Law Board issued a code of regulations on the subject, Guardians have been allowed to board children out at the homes of labouring people for a sum not to exceed 4s. weekly. As the "undertakings" signed by these foster parents only amounted to 535 last year, it seems probable that a plan which cannot be defended on any sound principles of Poor Law,[1] and which might lead to serious consequences as regards

---

[1] See some remarks by Mr. Fawcett, M.P., in his book on Pauperism.

parental responsibility, will not, owing to the cost and other difficulties attending it, become very general. The evidence in favour of the working of the school system is strong enough to prevent apprehension as to its results, and if removed from workhouses the schools would resemble the institutions in which so many children are educated by charity. And if the kindly feelings of the country were touched by the fact that the school is the only home that pauper children know, it would not be difficult to give them a holiday elsewhere as a reward for good conduct. It is not, however, to be supposed that improvements are not both needed and also being tried. At Birmingham, for instance, the new schools are divided into "homes" or separate cottages, built to contain thirty children each, and it is proposed to give a thorough industrial training. Meanwhile there is satisfactory evidence that even under the present indefensible system of schools in workhouses the children turn out well. In one case, out of seventy girls sent from the school, in ten years only four were known to have turned out badly, and three more to have returned to the house—this returning to the house being a direct and much to be deprecated result of the present system. This state of things, the report thinks, may be taken as typical of most workhouse schools, and, "though not one to be contented with, far removed from entire failure" (Mr. Mozley's Report for 1880).

It is seldom, we venture to think, that the conditions of an important reform are so clearly laid down as are those for one which is now being discussed. This may be called the classification of houses instead of wards in each house. The case stands thus: Setting aside the

large towns, who can make their own arrangements, there
are, as we have seen, a large number of workhouses
scattered about in country districts, and more or less
empty.   To group these for, as has been proposed, each
county, setting one apart for each of the various classes
of inmates, and in all probability greatly decreasing the
number, would be a matter of no great practical difficulty.
It does not fall within our province to discuss the matter ;
but if provision of a separate establishment for children
could be made without further cost, it seems almost culpable to delay moving in the matter.   We may remark
that, owing to the suppression of some metropolitan
Unions, some steps have been taken in this direction :
thus the house at Poplar was set aside for able-bodied
paupers of indifferent antecedents.   And of course the
principle is established by the provision of county asylums,
into which cases of lunacy that cannot be managed in
the workhouse are remitted to the amount of some
38,000, as against some 16,000 who remain in the house.

In connection with the subject of pauper children may
be mentioned the present system of apprenticing, which
shows the Poor Law at its best.   In place of that old and
melancholy drudge, the parish apprentice, boys are now
sent off fairly well taught and prepared to employers who
are glad to have them.   Every care is taken by the
regulations to secure proper treatment, and it is a duty
specially cast upon the Guardians to see to the welfare
of those whom they apprentice.   A particularly pleasant
part of the system is to be found in a circular of the
Local Government Board, transmitting to the Guardians
copies of the regulations for entering the Royal Navy,
" their lordships having been given to understand that

there are many boys in the Unions throughout the country who may be eligible and also wish to enter the service." Considering the attractions of the Royal Navy, it is probable that few have been able to avail themselves of the offer; but the spirit shown in making it, and its tendency to bridge over the gulf that divides the pauper from the citizen, by enabling the boy to defend his country instead of being maintained by it, is above praise.

There remains yet one other inmate of the workhouse, or rather of the special wards commonly attached to it, concerning whom something must be said. The regulations as to the treatment of "casual paupers" which is now the recognized title for "tramps" or "vagrants," are contained in a general order not yet ten years old (November 1871), and yet already, in the opinion of most Poor Law administrators, becoming in urgent need of alteration. Vagrants may be admitted into the casual wards by order of the relieving officer, by the master of a workhouse, or the superintendent of the ward; and in the Metropolis admission cannot be refused if the applicant is brought by a constable. The order of admission is available for one night only, and does not take effect earlier than six in the evening in winter, and eight in summer. The vagrant is searched and bathed, his clothes taken from him, and, if necessary, dried or disinfected. He is placed in a separate cell,[1] though the Central Board may as to this approve of other arrange-

---

[1] Young children are, of course, allowed to remain with their mother, and the writer remembers, as one of the saddest conceivable sights, a woman, whom the authorities believed to be quite respectable, and two handsome children crouching by her in a vagrant ward; it seemed as if she had reached the lowest depth of the misery of life.

ments, and is not entitled to discharge himself before
11 A.M. the next day, and then only if he has done the
task-work,—breaking stones, picking oakum, etc. etc.,—
which has been assigned to him. In the event of his
having become an inmate of the same ward twice in one
month, he may be detained till 9 A.M. of the third day
after admission. He receives 8 oz. of bread, or 6 oz. of
bread and one pint of gruel or broth, for supper and
breakfast.

There are not two opinions about the entire inefficacy
of the above arrangements, and that for the plain and
simple reason that they sin against the fundamental
principle of making the relieved person's condition worse
than that of the self-supporting labourer. To which
may be added the want of that great Poor Law weapon
of administration called classification; for it is impossible to distinguish between the honest labourer tramping
in search of work (though surely these ought to be few)
and the professional vagrant. To the latter the casual
ward is simply an arrangement that helps him to live
the rest of his life as pleases him best. The number relieved on any given day, say, for instance, January 1,
1881, when it was 6215, represents only a part (perhaps
one sixth) of a much larger body, who pass like a melancholy theatrical army over the stage in different detach-
ments. The rest of his time the habitual vagrant enjoys
life in his own way. He has his pleasures, his liberty, his
money, his opportunities of committing crime, and of ex-
tracting money from the bounty of a misguided public,
whom no expostulation will prevent from relieving what
appears at the moment to be genuine distress. In short,
the vagrant is still, as he has ever been, master of the posi-

tion—the scandal and standing difficulty of Poor Law administration. At the threat of mere punishment he laughs, as well knowing that it would but add force to his entreaty "for a piece of bread to save a poor fellow from having to go to jail."

The effect of a system which is neither remedial nor repressive, but which does little more than keep vagrancy alive, upon the character of the vagrants themselves, may be easily imagined. "The effect of this is to educate and confirm the pauper in vagrant habits, to destroy his self-respect, to lessen his physical powers and moral fitness for independent labour. Neither hard fare nor imprisonment have a deterring effect upon him now, and the 'I don't care,' or 'I wish I were dead,' betrays the condition of mind into which he has fallen. . . . His stay in the casual ward has been too short for any good influence to reach him."[1] It is surely a very serious matter that there should be many thousands of persons in such a country as ours of whom such a description should be possible.

Some of the remedies for this distressing state of things that have been suggested are as follows :—The "Dorset system" of repressing indiscriminate alms-giving by a plan of giving bread-tickets, which has succeeded in that county; putting vagrancy under the control of the police; making habitual vagrancy a penal offence, which would imply the establishment of correctional workhouses as part of a new classification of houses. It is, however, probable that much more information, such as could be obtained only by a com-

[1] Paper read at the Central Conference of Guardians by Mr. Vallance in 1880.

mission of enquiry as to their numbers, habits, and proceedings, would be required before the matter is ripe for legislation.[1]

PART V.—SETTLEMENT.

Settlement arose, as we have seen, from the idea that every parish was bound to maintain its own poor, and that every person was entitled to be considered as having a settlement in some one parish, to which, if he became destitute, he was chargeable, and could be removed to it. The Reform of 1834, while taking from the separate parishes the office of administering their own relief, did not take the further and obvious step (how illogical and undecisive is English legislation at its best!) of altering the place of settlement or area of chargeability, which still remained the parish. The same principle of devolving upon localities the task of providing for whatever paupers have become legally chargeable to them still obtains; but the system has been almost revolutionized by gradual changes in the area of the localities, and in the modes of becoming chargeable to them, which we will now proceed to point out.[2]

---

[1] It must not, however, be supposed that the community is any less responsible for the existence of the vagrant than of the pauper. So long as the homes of the working classes are what the State allows them to be, we are not entitled to be surprised that so many prefer to be homeless. At present the localities where workmen MUST live are most often covered with miserable houses quite unsuited for their purpose. The working people are able and willing to pay a rent that would cover the full value of the land and of proper habitations to be built upon it, but they cannot be expected to pay the cost of destroying the houses which previous neglect has allowed to accumulate. This is the duty of the State.

[2] To show how strong was the old idea that the area of the

The thin edge of the wedge was indeed introduced
in the Act of 1834 itself, by the formation of a common
fund in each Union for the payment of what are called
establishment charges—that is, the salaries of officers,
building and maintenance of the workhouse, and so on.
To this fund each parish contributed, not according to
its rateable value, but according to its expenditure in
poor relief. In 1846 some alteration in the law of
settlement in the interests of the working people, who
were still bound to their own parishes, was found to be
necessary, and a very important Act, called the Irremovable Poor Act, was passed, by which it was provided that
persons who had lived five years in one parish should not
be removed from it, but become chargeable to it so long
as residence was maintained.   It will be observed that
residence does not confer a settlement in the sense that
the pauper could claim relief if he left the parish, and
became chargeable elsewhere, in which case he would
have to fall back upon his original earlier settlement
by birth, or otherwise.   The same Act also forbade the
removal of widows during the first year, of children
under sixteen, unless their parents are removed with
them, and of cases of sickness when the sickness was not
such as to cause permanent destitution.   It seems almost
impossible to those who are unacquainted with the
phenomena of English legislation that Parliament did
not perceive, what of course immediately happened, that
the burden thrown upon the parishes in which the irre-
relieving locality should be small, as contrasted with the modern
idea that it should be as large as possible, we may mention that
large old parishes, especially in the north of England, were broken
up into townships and hamlets, each with its own overseer, and
liability to provide for its own paupers.

movables were residing would become a source of serious hardship. Next year, therefore, an Act was passed to remedy this injustice by throwing the cost of such irremovables upon the Union; and so the very important modification of substituting union for parochial chargeability came into existence almost by chance.

Once, however, that the principle was introduced, it spread gradually over other parts of the Poor Law system. In 1848 the relief and burial of destitute way-farers was cast upon the common fund. In 1861 the time of residence by which a pauper might acquire the status of irremovability was diminished from five years to three, and the area was extended from one parish to the whole Union. At the same time, it was enacted that parishes should contribute to the common fund, not, as heretofore, according to their expenditure in poor relief, but according to their rateable value. And finally, in 1865, the substitution of union for parochial chargeability was completed by enacting that the cost of the whole poor relief of the Union should be charged upon the common fund, while at the same time settlement was almost virtually abolished for practical purposes by the provision that residence for one year should make a pauper chargeable to the Union where he was residing.

In 1867, and again in 1870, the Metropolis was specially dealt with. London, it must be remembered, though divided for administrative purposes into as many as thirty Unions, is practically one city, so that the division into Unions, some at the extreme of poverty, and others of wealth, operates very unfairly upon the ratepayers, who are all members of one immense com-

munity.   Accordingly steps were taken which practically amounted to making London one large Union for
certain special purposes.   A common fund was created
by contributions from the various Unions, upon which
was charged the cost of district asylums for the relief of
the sick and insane, dispensaries, vaccination, and other
matters ; while, by the later Act, indoor relief to the
amount of 5d. per day was also charged upon the same
fund, thereby holding out two much needed inducements
—first, to extend indoor accommodation in the London
houses ; second, to practise economy in the giving of
out-relief, which was still left to be defrayed by each
Union.   The financial effect of this reform may be
estimated from the fact that up to 1879 Bethnal Green
Union had gained £200,946, and the City of London
had paid £445,720.   The annual gain of the first Union
is now about £20,000, and the loss of the latter about
£60,000.   The rest of the Unions gain or lose of course
according to their rateable value.

The whole question is, however, at this moment once
more re-opened.   A Committee of the House of Commons
in 1879 expressed a preference for the Irish system, where
there is no power of removal, and reported that settlement should be disregarded except for persons landing
in a destitute condition at seaport towns.   They recognized that settlement operates as a test of pauperism, and
also prevents burdens being thrown upon large towns,
where persons would become chargeable who had no
interest or permanent residence in the district.   Against
this they set the argument that settlement is wrong in
principle, inasmuch as it impedes the circulation of
labour ; that hardships from unfair removals still take

place; that litigation would be avoided. And they
conclude, in words that must sound ominous to those who
know what legislation thought and said and did not a
hundred years ago, "that the question should be regarded,
not merely in the supposed interest of the ratepayer,
but with sympathy and care for the convenience and
material advantage of the 'poor'"—(See *Report of Local
Government Board for* 1880, p. 43.)

But before a final step is taken it will have to be
seriously considered that the case of Ireland is nothing
to the purpose, for in that country, if there is no settlement, so also is there no out-relief. Since indoor relief
is virtually guaranteed by the State to all who, accepting the test, choose to avail themselves of it, it is of no
great importance, except for convenience of administration, where the indoor pauper is relieved, or over what
area he becomes chargeable. His settlement might very
properly be "national," and the area of chargeability
either a national common fund (as in the Metropolis),
or the county and large towns. But if the consequences
apprehended by the Committee came to pass, namely,
that there was an undue influx of paupers into certain
places, and if, following the precedents of recent legislation, the area of chargeability for out-relief was also
increased because of the injustice done to these places,
there is good reason for apprehending a large increase in
outdoor pauperism and much laxness of administration
in a sphere where laxness is already sufficiently conspicuous. Relieving authorities will vote money freely
when it is not raised from their own localities, and the
supervision, knowledge, and investigation so essential to
any reasonable administration of out-relief would become

impossible. This is but one of the many dangers, in some respects, if we bear in mind our changed social, economical, and political condition, the *growing* dangers, to which the existence of the Poor Law exposes the nation. In view of which it is earnestly to be hoped that " citizens " will study these very serious questions in all their bearings, historical, moral, and industrial, for themselves. It is to help them in this duty that this handbook has been planned and written, the object being to lay before the reader such facts as seemed most needed to inform his mind and guide his judgment.

CHAPTER VI.

POOR LAW STATISTICS.

No history of Poor Law would be complete that did not give some statistical account of the progress of administration under the new Act. Out of the enormous mass of figures and calculations at our disposal, there are, however, but comparatively few that are of interest to the "citizen," who is concerned only with broad and general results. We will begin with a comparative statement of the cost and extent of pauperism for every tenth year since 1834. Unfortunately the last census year is not yet available for our purpose, and the population is therefore estimated. It must be remembered that the number of paupers is the mean number between those returned as receiving relief on the 1st of January and 1st of July in each year, and does not therefore represent the total number of recipients in each year.

Year.	Population.	Expenditure.	Per head of Pop.	Paupers.	Per cent of Pop.[1]
			s. d.		
1834	14,372,000	£6,317,255	8 9½		
1841	15,911,757	4,760,929	5 11¾	1,299,048(?)	7·5(?)
1851	17,927,609	4,962,704	5 6½	941,315	5·3
1861	20,066,224	5,778,943	5 9	883,921	4·4
1871	22,712,266	7,886,724	6 11¼	1,037,360	4·6
1880	25,323,000	8,015,010	6 4	808,030	3·2

[1] This is calculated upon a rather smaller population, inasmuch as a few places, e.g. the Scilly Isles, make no return of paupers.

The results of this Table, so far as they disclose both an absolute and relative decrease in the number of paupers, may be pronounced moderately satisfactory, although the total number of paupers is still alarmingly great. Nor is the satisfaction (such as it is) sensibly abated by the increased expenditure, when we remember the far larger increase in the value of rateable property, and also that the total amount now covers large sums expended in improved methods of administration, *e.g.* the care of lunatics, and the cost of buildings of all sorts. The lowest rate ever reached was 2.9 in 1878, which was all the more remarkable, inasmuch as it was a reduction from 4.7 in 1870, when laxness of administration had led to very bad results.

The next Table contains the mean number of indoor, outdoor, and also able-bodied paupers for each year, and the actual number of lunatics and vagrants on the 1st of January for the same years. The enumeration of lunatics in asylums (classed as outdoor) only began in 1859, and partly accounts for the increase after that year.

Year.	Indoor.	Outdoor.	Able-bodied.	Lunatics.	Vagrants.
1841	192,106	1,109,642	...	...	...
1851	114,367	826,948	163,124	14,346	3390
1861	125,866	758,055	145,776	32,887	1941
1871	156,430	880,930	172,460	48,334	3735
1880	180,817	627,213	115,785	61,295	5914

The first three columns display some gradual improvement, while, what is perhaps a more hopeful sign, the decrease upon the last decade shows how entirely the growth of pauperism, as shown in 1871, was due to mere

culpable carelessness of administration, and how easy it
is to abate the disease by proper remedies, such as discussion, conferences, and painstaking zeal, can suggest.
The increased number of indoor paupers only practically means that a larger number of impotent folk
have obtained a better mode of living than they could
have had if they had remained outside the house, upon
the supposition, that is, that they had failed from neglect
or incapacity to provide for themselves. The same may
be said more emphatically of the insane, though the
Table points to a growth of insanity amongst us, and also
to a growing inclination on the part of persons, who
ought to know better, to put off the care of their insane
relatives upon the State. And it is a serious question
how far subventions by the State lead to laxness of
administration. The increase of vagrants has been
alluded to before, and demands immediate attention.

A question of great interest arises as to the local distribution of pauperism ; but, unfortunately, the want of
calculations based upon the census of 1881 prevents us
from giving any but very general results. The next
Table gives the amount of indoor and outdoor pauperism,
together with the ratio of cost for 1880, in each of the
eleven Poor Law districts, on January 1, 1881. The
population is that of 1871, and it will be understood
that the superiority of the urban and less pauperized
districts will be further enhanced by the shifting of
population into those districts.

Division.	Population.	Indoor Paupers.	Outdoor.	Total.	Percentage of cost of Outdoor.
Welsh . . .	1,420,213	6,760	61,060	67,820	84·9
S.-Western .	1,879,925	12,567	75,394	87,961	78·0
Northern . .	1,365,041	7,782	34,166	41,948	70·7
N.-Midland .	1,406,911	8,319	37,045	45,364	70·0
S.-Midland .	1,443,716	11,739	49,312	61,051	69·5
Eastern . .	1,218,726	9,861	42,674	52,535	69·4
York . . .	2,444,592	13,866	60,395	74,261	68·3
W.-Midland .	2,721,931	22,311	79,855	102,166	62·5
S.-Eastern .	2,164,219	20,944	59,193	80,137	56·7
N.-Western .	3,388,399	28,327	64,090	92,417	50·6
Metropolis .	3,252,629	52,810	50,871	103,681	27·9

The general result of this Table is to show that, subject to modification from local peculiarities, e.g. of trade or character, the tendency is for those Unions who spend most in out-relief to be the most heavily burdened by pauperism. But the essential imperfection of the present system is most clearly revealed if we compare the results which obtain in different Unions, and find, as we shall do, that the proportion of paupers to population ranges from about 14 to about 75 per 1000 (i.e. more than five times as much), and also that the outdoor pauperism is in one case 4 per 1000, and in others (at any rate in one other) 71 per 1000. The Union thus honourably distinguished is, as all Poor Law authorities are aware, that of Atcham in Shropshire (including now Shrewsbury), where a long course of careful attention to the proper principles of Poor Law administration has brought pauperism down to what it might, by equal care, be brought nearly all over England,—population 45,565 ; indoor paupers, 426 ; outdoor, 196 ; total, 622. To this we may add that there are several instances in which, by the exercise of a little trouble, outdoor pauperism has been reduced 50 per cent[1] in a few years without causing any known or appreciable hardship. And the returns disclose the most striking variations in Unions that lie perhaps side by side, or are not distinguishable from each other in respect of population, wealth, or industrial occupation. And when we remember how deeply such variations penetrate into the lives and characters of the working classes, and into the taxation and prosperity of the district, the matter assumes a very serious aspect.

The following additional items may be interesting.

The expenditure for the year 1880 was divided thus :—

In Maintenance.	Out-Relief.	Lunatic Asylums, etc.	Workhouse and other loans.	Salaries, etc.	Other Expenses.
£ 1,757,749	£ 2,710,778	£ 994,204	£ 319,426	£ 1,053,218	£ 1,181,511

The officers were as follows :—clerks, 624; medical officers, 4030; masters, 651; relieving officers, 1,387. Of these apparently between 100 and 200 are dismissed or obliged to resign every year.

The following is a complete list of all the institutions in which indoor paupers may now be maintained. Some of them are, however, to be found only in the metropolis. Workhouse, infirmary, lunatic asylum, fever hospital, smallpox hospital, convalescent home, separate (Union) school, district school, certified school, institution for

[1] In some East London Unions the decrease has been far greater.

deaf and dumb or blind, training-ship. The number of children in average attendance at the workhouse (including separate) schools was 27,939; at the district schools, 7070; in the training-ship *Exmouth*, 214 ;—total, 35,223.

Conferences of Guardians are now held annually in many districts, and are strongly encouraged by the Central Board. To them may be attributed some part of the undoubted improvement that has taken place in the last ten years in the administration of relief.

In bringing the epitome of the history and operations of English Poor Law to a conclusion, it may be proper to indicate more precisely the questions which the course of our inquiry has suggested, as requiring the particular and immediate attention of public opinion with a view to future reforms. They are these—

I. Can anything be done to reduce pauperism by correcting the gross disparity between outdoor and indoor relief; it being remembered that the former (*a*) constitutes a burden upon real property to the extent of between £3,000,000 and £4,000,000 per annum; (*b*) acts as a protective duty in favour of the labourer as against the farmer, and in favour of the farmer (or landlord) as against the ratepayer; (*c*) inflicts, as all protection must do, serious injury upon the labouring class, who are, in the case of the agricultural labourer, kept in a state of tutelage and dependence, and who are the first to suffer from any interference with the natural relations of labour and capital?

II. Can anything be done to classify and arrange workhouses, so as to make them more fit for different classes of inmates, and also save expense?

M

III. Can anything be done to repress vagrancy and
self-inflicted pauperism by resorting to correctional discipline ?

IV. Can nothing be done to remove children from
pauperizing associations, even though this might lead to
withdrawing them from the control of unworthy parents ?

V. Can anything be done to stimulate local interest
and secure supervision by an improved system of municipal government ?

VI. Can anything be done to place the relations
between Poor Law and Charity upon a sounder and
more reasonable footing ?

In discussing these serious and interesting questions,
the great truth, which has come out, if possible, clearer
than any other, must steadily be remembered, that State
relief of the indigent is a necessary part of civilized social
life, and that they mistake the conditions of the problem
who regard it as a temporary episode, or as something
peculiar to ourselves.   Pauperism may be almost in-
definitely modified, and the modes of giving relief are
capable of much improvement, but the thing itself must
in some shape or other ever remain : the poor we shall
have always with us.   Perhaps the most striking con-
firmation of the necessity of Poor Law is to be found in
the words of one of the greatest of modern thinkers,
whose opinion is all the more valuable because the subject seems at first sight far removed from the range of
topics with which he usually occupied himself, and with
which his name is commonly identified :—" Men are
likewise overcome by liberality ; chiefly those who have
not wherewithal to buy the necessaries of life.   But

helping every one in need is far beyond the means and convenience of any private person. For a private man's wealth is no match for such a demand. Also a single man's opportunities are too narrow for him to contract friendship with all. Wherefore, providing for the poor is a duty that falls on the whole community, and has regard only to the common interest."—SPINOZA.[1]

[1] *Life and Philosophy*, by Frederick Pollock, page 273.

APPENDIX.

THE POOR LAW IN 1890.

SINCE the first edition of this book ten years have elapsed, and it would seem natural to inquire what changes have been made and what fresh results established. A comparatively easy task, for there is next to nothing to record. It is true, indeed, that the results of the Reform of 1885 are beginning slowly to be felt in the altered ways of regarding the Poor Law, in some minor alterations, and in some preposterous proposals. But on the whole we find the same difficulties, faults, remedies, and statistics; Acts of Parliament deal with the old subjects, which conferences year after year discuss with comparatively little fresh information or new ideas. It is well worth realizing that, for the moment, the Poor Law is of all great English institutions the most thoroughly stereotyped, and yet that there are not wanting signs of a spirit, naturally resulting from the democratic movement, which may greatly modify—perhaps for good—Poor Law administration, or may equally well, if not carefully watched, end in great disaster.

Let us begin our comparison with some of the more important statistical returns :—

	1880.	Report for 1889.
Expenditure	£8,015,010	£8,440,821
Per head of population . .	6s. 3¾d.	5s. 11¾d.
Paupers—Indoor . . .	180,817	192,105
Outdoor . . .	627,213	603,512
Total	808,030	795,617
Able-bodied . .	115,785	98,817
Lunatics . . .	63,470	75,581
Vagrants . . .	5,914	7,058
Per cent of population (in 1000) .	31·8	27·8

The different districts and counties still retain much the same positions. Wales is still the worst in respect of the proportion of out-relief; the South Western in respect of the total number, reaching the terrible amount of 41·9 per 1000. Dorset heads the list with 48·4 per 1000; Lancashire closes it with 19·3 per 1000; but the real place of honour is still held by Shropshire with 21·5, or not one-half of Dorset, both alike being agricultural counties. This alone would be enough to prove (though proof has for long been needless) that all the causes which affect the growth or decrease of pauperism, *e.g.* bad times, high prices, are as nothing compared with the effects of good or bad administration. As surely as different localities depend for their death-rate upon their sanitary administration, so surely does their pauperism depend upon the way in which the Guardians discharge their duties. Man cannot destroy pauperism any more than he can destroy death; he can if he pleases reduce both to their lowest possible terms.

We shall now sum up the scanty alterations in the Poor Law under the head of the six questions with which we closed the last chapter.

I. *The Proportion between Outdoor and Indoor Relief.*— Here, as the figures just given plainly show, there has been slight though real progress. The report says: "Another noticeable and very satisfactory feature in connection with the decrease in pauperism is, that whilst the ratio of outdoor paupers to population was less in 1889 than in any of the forty preceding years, the number of indoor paupers, as compared with population, was also smaller in 1889 than in any year since 1879." The ratio of indoor paupers has fallen from 7·7 per 1000 in 1849 to 6·7 in 1889; but outdoor paupers during the same period have fallen from 55 to 21·1. Against this must be set the increase in the number of pauper lunatics, concerning whom, it may be noticed, a humane Act was passed in 1886 providing for their reception in hospitals, institutions, and licensed houses with a view to their education and training. But no part of Poor Law expenditure is less to be grudged than this, and the increase in numbers, we may hope, merely indicates that resort is more freely had to the superior care and treatment which the State can give to these unhappy ones.

It must, however, be confessed that the inspectors' reports show little improvement and much fault in the actual administration of the Poor Law by the Guardians; and the number of unions which have attained to anything like satisfactory results is still very few. Moreover, the cry for out-relief with all the old fallacious reasons has increased rather than abated with the enfranchisement of the country labourer. But we are convinced that his common sense will soon reject the appeal to his good nature which it suits his political leaders to address to him, when he discovers that pauperism made easy is one of the most dangerous enemies the cause of labour has to contend against.

II. *The Classification of Houses.*—Under this head nothing, so far as we know, has been attempted. It will obviously require some change in the area of administration, and in the constitution of the local authorities, to which attention will be called presently.

III. *Vagrancy.*—In 1882 was passed the Casual Poor Act with the intention of stopping the increase of vagrancy. The main point was that the casual could not discharge himself from the Ward till nine o'clock on the second day, instead of eleven the first day, nor before he had performed the prescribed work. If he presented himself twice at the same ward within one month he could be detained until the fourth day. But nothing seems of any avail. In London the total admissions fell at once under the new Act from 294·960 to 125·906, but it now stands at 241·958. The mean number of vagrants relieved in England and Wales was in 1882 6·114; it fell in 1883 to 4·790, but rose in 1889 to 6·504. The relaxation of rules as regards detention and laxity in the enforcement of proper work is set down as accounting for the increase. The difficulty of discrimination between the honest wayfarer and the professional tramp remains as it was and always has been, and the warfare of some 600 years between the vagrant and society continues still to be waged to the advantage of the former. The casual ward, while it affords a certain sort of relief under tremendous penalties to the honest man, is to the tramp only a last resource at times when he can do no better for himself—which, thanks to private charity, he generally can. It is, after all, only another form of the everlasting outdoor relief question, and the vagrant gets the better of society only because human nature, so far at any rate, cannot resist the plea of sentiment when presented, not in the person of some one locally known to be undeserving, but in the guise of an interesting stranger with an affecting story,—which may possibly be true.   It is just possible that things might be improved if the casual was taken out of Poor Law and put under a special department of the police, but that would press terribly hard upon the better class of wanderers, unless, indeed, means could be found of relegating them to charity organization.   The wards established by religious agencies, together with the meals, meetings, and addresses, are almost certainly productive of much harm.

IV. *Children and pauperizing Associations.*—In connection with this all-important matter I put the question in 1880, " Can nothing be done to remove children from pauperizing associations, even though this might lead to withdrawing them from the control of unworthy parents?" and in 1890 I have the great satisfaction of recording that this step has been at last taken.   The Act of 1889 provides that when any child is—having been deserted—maintained by the Guardians, the Guardians may resolve to assume parental control over boys till the age of sixteen, and over girls till eighteen, till which time the powers and rights of parents vest in the Guardians.   Imprisonment for offences against children is counted for desertion.   The "resolve" of the Guardians may be rescinded voluntarily if they think fit, or by a court of law at the instance of the parents, if they can make out a case.   The parent's liability to contribute to the maintenance of his children remains as it was, even though the Guardians exercise parental control.   This, of course, as a matter of principle, is as it should be, but it may be doubted whether in actual experience it will have much effect, except indeed as a deterrent.

Thus is removed from Poor Law administration a most serious reproach.   Previously Guardians were compelled on demand to give up to the so-called care of most unworthy parents children whom they had maintained and educated in decency and morality.   A more distressing spectacle than that of young children reclaimed all at once by some villain

who had deserted them, and wandering away by his side into
misery and vice, can hardly be imagined, and that it should
have been suffered to continue till 1889 attests the wonderful
slowness of English legislation in working out logical results
in practice. Cruelty and desertion were hardly so injurious
to children as reclamation when they were old enough to be
useful for vicious purposes. The "right divine to govern
wrong" has lingered with parents long after it has been taken
away from other classes of persons in authority, who have
had to be taught that after all a man may not do exactly
what he likes even with his own.

Thus begins a new and in every way satisfactory chapter
in the history of Poor Law; and we have little doubt that it
is owing to measures of this kind, supplemented by others
outside the Poor Law, and greatly helped by the growth of
voluntary rescue work of young children, that the great improvement in the statistics of crime has taken place—an
improvement for which mere education gets far more than
its due credit. There remains, however, much yet to be
done, and we may just mention the matter of insurance of
young children, which has some relation to Poor Law objects,
though, of course, not within its scope. It is provoking to
think that thrift should take this unlovely form, and that
the persistent efforts of interested speculation should draw
from the pockets of working people immense sums which the
best-directed philanthropy fails to reach. As a testimony,
however, to the superiority of voluntary and individual effort
over State interference it is not without its value; still the
State must interfere at times on behalf of the weak, and if
ever there was a case, this is one in which the State might
say, "If, instead of providing for the life of your children,
you prefer to provide for their death, we will take care that
you shall do it through us and under strict supervision." It
is a bad business full of evil omen for the future.

So far for an attempt to improve the Poor Law in respect
of the care of children by scientific method; now let us turn
to an attempt in which sentiment and not principle is the
ruling spirit. In the first edition, p. 144, a very guarded
opinion was expressed about the system of boarding out
children in the homes of (so-called) foster-parents, and the

prediction was hazarded that it " will not, owing to the cost and other difficulties attending it, become very general." This very harmless prophecy aroused a current of indignation which flashed into light so far away as the colony of Victoria, which had just adopted *in toto* the boarding-out system.[1] This is not the place to continue the controversy thence ensuing, and contained in the Reports of the Colonial Department; but, so far as our own country is concerned, I am delighted to be able to say that the prophecy as to increase has come true, and sincerely grieved at being obliged to add that the evils predicted have come true also.

The number of boarded-out children is returned as only 3,996 as opposed to 53,815 receiving indoor relief, 29,694 being returned as the average attendance at school, yet even in this limited area abuses have already taken firm root. The evidence for this is contained in the interesting and candid report of Miss Mason, the lady appointed by the Local Government Board as Inspector of boarded-out children, whose testimony is all the more convincing because she remains of the same opinion as to the "excellence of the boarding-out system, if accompanied by supervision which is both thorough and adequate,"—the said supervision, be it remembered, being of maternal duties in the daily details of home life, scattered

[1] It may be well to reproduce from the Report of the Department for Neglected Children in Victoria a few sentences from the letter to which the Secretary's letter defending the boarding-out system was an answer. It seems to me to sum up the essence of the objections that may be urged against it. I wrote as follows : "The Report for 1884 says that 'a majority of the children are probably much better cared for under the boarding-out system than children of the same class by their own parents.' If it were in my power I should like to commend this simple sentence to the consideration of every working-class taxpayer in Victoria, and I should like to help him to the due appreciation of its meaning by the following illustration. Let us suppose a row of twenty houses occupied by working people of the same class. At one end of the scale is a very respectable childless couple, whose circumstances are much above the average, though they live by the same employment as the others. At the other end is a worthless couple with a large family of children, who for one cause or another become paupers. The effect of the boarding-out system practically is that the remaining eighteen families pay their well-to-do neighbour for bringing up the children of their badly-disposed neighbour at a greater cost than they can afford for their own."

about in country districts. Here are a few of the results of the supervision admirably "thorough and adequate" which Miss Mason has exercised.

"Boarding out has become so popular a hobby, and there is so much disposition to overlook unsatisfactory facts, that a strong warning is necessary for the protection of children (p. 157, Local Government Board Report for 1889).

"I have found some of the best and worst homes together at the same time under the same Committee. This shows that what is satisfactory is due to the kindness of particular foster-parents, not to the selection and supervision of the homes by the Committees." In plain words, the happiness of children for whom the community has made itself responsible depends upon mere chance.

"The labouring class do not trust boarding out as a system. They regard it on the whole as a means of gain to the foster-parents. I find jealousy in abundance, not of the children, but of the foster-parents who have been lucky enough to obtain the payments.

"One of the best foster-mothers said to me, 'I would rather see my own child in her grave than boarded out.'

"Untruths about the children's sleeping arrangements have often been told me by foster-parents who have sometimes deceived the Committees in this matter," and in one case "I saw the woman signal to the boarded-out boy to be silent."

Perhaps the most unsatisfactory feature of the whole is the fact that persons recommend foster-parents out of charity to them and as a means of living. One gentleman recommended a disabled coachman and his wife, who received 32s. a week (besides extras) for eight children. A clergyman recommended an old schoolmistress. The "great lady of the place" had insisted upon sending children to an unsatisfactory home as a means of providing for her dependants.

Thus then the boarding-out system has revealed and called into exercise some of the worst faults to which human nature—from great ladies to poor widows—is liable. Deception, jealousy, greed, neglect of duty by irresponsible Committees, selfish good-nature, that secret unkindness which is so much more dangerous than open cruelty, in short, all the

evils which have attended the history of Poor Law relief are
discovered by one Inspector flourishing in the case of some
4000 children, or rather of the percentage of them that were
inspected.   The report almost carries one back to the days
of 1834.   It is no answer to say, even if it were true, that a
considerable number of children get better treatment than
they would do at district schools, or for the matter of that,
in the ordinary homes of working people.   It is the exceptions, the very numerous exceptions, of those who are sacrificed in the lottery for the good of the others that constitute
the charge against the State that permits it.   Every such
ill-treated child has, so to speak, good cause of action against
its true foster-parent, the State itself, which has delegated
its duties to irresponsible persons, and in trying to put
destitute children in a better position than the children of
parents who support them, has only ended in the inevitable
result thus described in the words of the Report (p. 160):
"I do not say that the children were ill-treated or neglected
in all such cases.   I only wish to draw attention to the
dangers arising from the fact that, according to my experience, the benefit of the children themselves is not always
the primary object of boarding them out, and that the great
majority of the foster-parents take them for the sake of
profit."

V. *Improved Local Government.*—It is at this point that the
direct results of the late Reform Act are beginning to be
felt, and great changes seen to be imminent.   County councils
are already established, and the restoration of village
government, that great act of wisdom and justice, is almost
assured.   Again a lurking suspicion is beginning to betray
itself as to value of government by artificial unhistoric
districts—that is as independent separately elected authorities.   It is at least certain that government by districts has
never flourished anywhere out of England, and in England
only as a reaction from the old Poor Law, and in default of
government by counties and communes.   And it may well
be that Unions are destined to go the way of Hundreds, and
be retained only for subsidiary purposes of administration.

Why should not each county be responsible for its own
Poor Relief?   It might be necessary to except certain large

towns, which, *e.g.* Cambridge, though not counties themselves, are too important and too distinct from rural Unions
to be associated with them for Poor Law administration.
What would be gained first of all would be uniformity of
treatment. In Oxfordshire, for instance, there is (I have
not the exact figures) a disparity between precisely similar
Unions in the number of paupers of nearly 100 per cent.
Now this cannot be right, and upon the face of it must be
most unfair to the working people or to the ratepayer, or
more probably to both. Therefore there should be county
control to correct mere differences of administration.

Next, are there to be district councils elected by popular
vote, with the power of granting or withholding outdoor
relief? It is as certain as anything can be that this question
would dominate and vitiate all local politics ; and even those
who, like myself, have the greatest confidence in the common
sense of working people, might well distrust the effects of a
popular cry, "Vote for so-and-so and outdoor relief." Of
course ultimately this, like every other question, must be
decided by popular vote, but if it took its place simply
among a number of other questions of general county and
political interest, the evils likely to result from direct voting
upon the subject of poor relief would be much diminished.
It would follow from this that the Unions would continue
to exist only as subdivisions of the county, and would
be administered by committees of the county council
chosen from the district, but with powers delegated by the
county to which they would be responsible. That the active
administrators of Poor Law should be as far removed as
possible from actual contact with the voting classes, provided the principle of local government is steadily adhered
to, may be set down as almost an axiom of poor law
management, and the interposition of the county seems in
every way exactly fitted to fulfil this condition.

VI. *Poor Law and Charity Organization.*—Upon this
subject it is only possible to say that upon the whole there
is some progress towards the still remote ideal when Poor
Law shall deal with destitution as such, and charity shall
take in hand the improvement of the condition of the working poor together with such relief, either supplementing or

superseding the Poor Law, as may by arrangement be allotted
to it. We may, however, just allude to a notable instance
of confusion between the two systems which is attracting
attention, and may perhaps lead to useful reforms. By their
gratuitous outdoor relief the London hospitals are doing
Poor Law work out of charitable resources, and by voluntary
agencies. Applicants for medical aid virtually plead destitution, are taken at their own word, and relieved without
further inquiry, the hospitals, in fact, reproducing for good or
evil the methods of the monasteries before Poor Law came
into existence. As might have been for certain predicted,
the departure from right principle leads to most unsatisfactory
results, recalling once more in a mitigated form the vices of
the old Poor Law. On the one hand medical aid is asked
for where it is not wanted, or where the applicant could
himself provide it ; on the other it is given in a superficial
and hasty fashion, without gratitude on the one part or
personal interest on the other. The subject is full of difficulties, trivial, however, in comparison with those which Parliament faced and overcame in 1834. It is to be hoped that
the present inquiry will lead to similar good results, but we
fear the temper of the public mind is not what it was in
those golden days of scientific reform.

Upon the whole, however, we may look forward to the future
of Poor Law with reasonable confidence that correct principles
will prevail. The working people are sure to discover, as
other classes have done before them, that unrestricted relief is,
if possible, more hurtful to the interests of labour than to those
of capital, employers, or the community itself. No doubt there
is much natural dissatisfaction both with the large number
of paupers together with the tardy decrease in that number,
and also with the condition to which paupers are *ipso facto*
reduced ; this last temper was shown very clearly in the
unwise enactment that medical relief should not temporarily
disfranchise the person who received it. This dissatisfaction
is itself good, and though it may lead to many illusory
suggestions, yet in the long run men will discover that there
is no royal road, such as National Insurance or the like, to
the extinction of pauperism, but that it must be done, if done
at all, by making work and thrift preferable to the pauper's

life, by gradual improvement in the material conditions and spiritual determinations of the lowest strata of the working classes, and especially by the growth of voluntary combinations for purposes of mutual help and support. We are not without hope that, as the relations between labour and capital become better adjusted, and the former is set more free to attend to its own internal interests, the Trades Unions will find themselves more and more able to act as substitutes for that other Union which has played so significant, so sad, and withal so necessary a part in the history of English industry. Then, and not till then, will the legitimate triumph of labour be achieved, and its long warfare at last accomplished.

A disturbing influence may perhaps be found in the growth of socialism, of whose future it is difficult to make a forecast. In connection with this it may, however, be well to clear the mind of one of the most foolish fallacies ever set agoing, viz. that the Poor Law is itself socialistic, and therefore that we need only to advance a little further in that direction. Poor Law is, in fact, the exact antithesis to socialism, or, more correctly, it acts as a safety valve expressly designed to allow the forces of competition to work at full pressure without danger of explosion. Socialism claims for each man, qua human, a full share in the common good ; Poor Law affords to man, qua destitute, a maintenance under conditions lowering to his humanity and below the average of his fellows : there is no abstract reason why socialism may not be right if it adheres to its own methods, but socialism working by Poor Law agencies or motives is a contradiction in terms. Still, it must be admitted that the democracy are not unlikely to be assailed at the instance of ignorant or unscrupulous agitators with the temptation to remedy or palliate the inequalities of life by means of indiscriminate relief. Against this must be set the fact that the knowledge of what Poor Law abuses have been and have wrought in the past is a strong specific against the recurrence of the same abuses in the future. Economical relapses are after all rare in the history of mankind.

THE END.

www.ingramcontent.com/pod-product-compliance
Lightning Source LLC
Chambersburg PA
CBHW020537270326
41927CB00006B/617